"A breath of fresh air... constraints seem to have the whip hand whenever it's my turn.... Lola writes in the first person with a simplicity that makes you feel good.... Her message is healthy, invigorating—may it free us from the ambient Jesuitism."
—Jean-Claude Leroy, *Mediapart*

"Lola lives revolt: anarchism, Situationist International, libertarian communism, 'outer left'... action committees, Women's Liberation Movement (MLF), Homosexual Revolutionary Action Front (FHAR), Gouines Rouges (Red Dykes), Les Gazolines.... Communal apartments, scandals, doing drugs (joints and acid—but no needles), *dérives*, living from odd jobs and expedients, drinking, making love/fucking (where was the dividing line?), networking, traveling to find friends and comrades (but no Hippie Trail to Kathmandu—that would be a copout), and ever ready for action but never lapsing into militantism ('the highest stage of alienation')."
—Gilles Dauvé, author of *Your Place or Mine? A 21st Century Essay on (Same) Sex*

"Now that everything is commercialized and our liberated zones have shriveled, this book of Lola's is a precious collection of recipes for freedom, a fine guide to combining political activism with personal liberation."
—Hélène Hazera

Fag Hag

Lola Miesseroff

Translated by Donald Nicholson-Smith

Afterword by Hélène Hazera

Fag Hag
Lola Miesseroff

English translation © 2023 by Donald Nicholson-Smith
This edition © 2023 PM Press
Originally published in French as *Fille à pédés*
© Éditions Libertalia, 2019
Translation arranged through Julie Finidori Agency

ISBN: 979-8-88744-010-1 (paperback)
ISBN: 979-8-88744-011-8 (ebook)
Library of Congress Control Number: 2023930800

Cover by John Yates / www.stealworks.com
Cover image from the February 1973 cover of *L'Antinorm*, published by the Homosexual Revolutionary Action Front (FHAR)
Interior design by briandesign

10 9 8 7 6 5 4 3 2 1

PM Press
PO Box 23912
Oakland, CA 94623
www.pmpress.org

Printed in the USA.

In memory of Pierre-Alban Berteloot
and Christian Pellegrini

Contents

Translator's Acknowledgments

I am deeply grateful, yet again, to Mia Nadezhda Rublowska, whose critical eye has improved this translation beyond measure. And to Lola Miesseroff's equally critical (and authorial) eye for catching a host of plain old mistakes. If translators had muses, these two would be mine. Cara Hoffman offered helpful suggestions, and John Simmons deployed his veteran's editorial punctilio, for which he has my warmest thanks. Jacqueline Reuss has been a great help to me as translator, as indeed she was to Lola all along.

D.N.-S., October 2021

A Distinctly Degendered Childhood

Most women have ordered or disordered childhoods. Mine I like to describe as "degendered." Born in the fall of 1947, I was not very properly initiated into the roles customarily assigned to the sexes. For one thing, I was coddled as a child by men. We lived in Marseille, where my mother, of Russian-Jewish heritage, was employed as a social worker by the Jewish Agency, while my father, whose background was Armenian and Russian, had set up a small sandpaper-manufacturing business in some wooden sheds abandoned as surplus by the Americans. So it was he who took care of me in the daytime. And when he couldn't, I was entrusted to Misha, a former Soviet soldier whom my parents had helped escape from Fort Saint-Jean, whence he was supposed to be repatriated to the USSR and in all likelihood sent to some Siberian prison camp. This Misha was a sweet man with an illness that was said to slow down his circulation and by extension all his movements and even his behavior. Which was probably what later on made him into such a first-rate breeder and trainer of wild animals for the Bouglione circus. I was proud of having had him as my nanny, especially when the circus came through Marseille and he took me to see his big cats. He would solemnly introduce me to each one, and if one dared growl, he would give it a good slap, saying, in Russian of course, "You be nice to Lola now. She was

Me aged four (spring 1952)

my baby before you were!" Once he wanted to give me an adorable lion cub; my parents refused flat out, which was only sensible but a bitter disappointment to me.

A couple of years later, my regular babysitter was Ahmed Salah Boulgobrah, known as Boule, sometime French army cook but now a resident of the nearby old folks' home and my best buddy. The only time I ever got angry with him was when he would not play Happy

Families with me, and I refused to believe that he couldn't read.

Having such offbeat nannies surely had something to do with my early confusion about gender. At about five, like many only children, I invented an imaginary country for myself and regaled all the adults around me with myriad details about it. In this fantasy land, I was the mother of two children, a boy called Monique and a girl called Richard, and woe betide anyone who tried to tell me that I must be mistaken: after all, surely I knew the first names of my own children! Apparently, by the way, those children lacked a father. I also invented a very dear friend, an opera singer named Aline Forêt. Being unable to spell, for I could not yet read or write, I would always explain her surname by adding "like *forêt*" (forest), but no doubt I had heard talk of Gabriel *Fauré*, whose nocturnes and barcaroles my father was forever playing on the piano.

True to the principle that no one betrays you more thoroughly than a friend, it was Aline who, albeit unwillingly (as if she possessed a will!), precipitated the destruction of my imaginary country. A woman friend of my mother's had conceived the perverse idea of sending me a holiday postcard signed "Aline Forêt." At first I refused to believe my mother, who had been delegated to read me the card, but my father vouched for the message and the signature. I flew into a towering rage, screaming that Aline couldn't have written anything because she did not exist. I simply wouldn't be calmed down, and nothing stemmed my tears. So, torpedoed by a grown-up's blunder, my imaginary country suddenly vanished forever, even if, like the mythical Breton town of Ys submerged in the ocean, it still wallows somewhere in a remote corner of my brain.

With my parents, Marseille, winter 1954

I reached my sixth birthday before I came to understand what it meant to be a girl. Naturally I was perfectly well acquainted with the anatomical differences between men and women, because my parents ran a naturist colony that was also our home. I could easily tell a *zizi* from a *zézette*—or, in Marseille parlance, a *chichi* from a *pachole*—even if my mother tended to use the ungendered Russian term *pipischka* for both. (The French equivalent would be *pissette*.) Having or not having one or the other didn't seem like a big deal to me. The kids at the colony all played together, and dolls, tea sets, marbles, and toy cars figured indiscriminately in our games. Neither boys nor girls had any separate activities, and we all romped about, played dodgeball, plunged into the swimming pool, and got into scraps as a single gang. Even when I was seven or eight, what I wanted for my birthday was a model railway. With their scant means, my parents could afford only a tiny Micheline train that went round and round in a circle, but for a while its three cars, with my dolls on the roof, were my pride and joy.

In 1953, just turned six, I went to school for the first time, joining the preparatory class of the girls' elementary school in the Lapin-Blanc neighborhood. There I discovered both girls' games and girl talk. I suddenly found myself playing hopscotch or jumping rope to the accompaniment of the song "*À la salade, je suis malade / Au céleri, je suis guérie*," words that left me perplexed: why should lettuce, which I liked, make me ill, and celery, which I hated, make me better? When it came to dancing in a circle and singing "Palais-Royal is a fine neighborhood / All the girls there are ready to wed," I had no idea at all what these girls were and what kind of weddings awaited them; I could hardly have read Restif de la Bretonne already and learnt that in our innocence we were serenading the whores in a red-light district!

It was mystifying, too, to hear the talk about boys, about who was in love with whom, who wanted to be the fiancée of this one or that—though of course the chosen one must know nothing of it. For my part, when I was only four my friend Kiki and I had planned to get married when we grew up.

I also discovered how charming little girls could be extraordinarily mean to one another: real fights were frequent, and the big sisters called upon to rescue their younger siblings seemed to me all the more formidable because I had no big sister of my own.

I was also confronted by racism, while quite ignorant of what it might be. I recall this only vaguely, but my mother was fond of reminding me that I once came home from school and brightly announced: "You know what, Mom, we don't play with the little Arab girls." To which she replied: "That's all well and good, but mark my words, if it's like that now, it will soon be the little Russian girls who nobody plays with." Her lesson was heard, she told me later, because the very next day I joined up with the Arab girls. Interestingly enough, the children of the school were, just like the neighborhood itself, ethnically diverse. There were very few straightforwardly French girls in my class, and no more North Africans than there were Italians, not to mention the Asians and those with Greek, Armenian, Yugoslavian, or Spanish names. My own name, being Russo-Armenian, was the only one of its kind. Who knows if some particular schoolgirlish conflict gave rise to the girls from the Maghreb being singled out. The fact is, though, that while no one was well-to-do, these girls were certainly the poorest of all, and the worst dressed, with some wearing sandals in the depths of winter.

That same year, I became aware that I had two first names and two last ones. Up until my first year of school, I could not read or write, but I had learnt to draw *LOLA* in block capitals, and that was how I signed my first drawing. When I handed it in, the teacher asked me who this Lola was, since my name was Hélène—which sounded only vaguely familiar to me. The Russians, just like the Spanish for that matter, love to use rather improbable diminutive names: thus, Yelena—Hélène in French and on my identification papers—became Lyena, Lyallya or Lyolya, rather as Alexander becomes Sasha, Shura, Sanya or Alyosha. My father, whose first name was Oxent, had, who knows why, been nicknamed "Alyosha" from earliest childhood, but in the family he was often called Lyolya, supposedly an abbreviation of Alyosha. I thus had a pet name that was gender-neutral in Russian, and I always wondered what had prompted him to pick a diminutive for me that was identical to his own as a little boy.

So I am officially Hélène, but for anyone even the slightest bit familiar with me I have always been Lola— the Frenchified form of Lyolya. I didn't like this one bit when I began my first year of junior high, nor later when I started working: I insisted on Hélène and thought Lola was vulgar. Only later did this duality allow me to separate myself, as Lola, from the Hélène ever so respectably employed.

The teacher who asked who Lola was must have been mystified, because she also asked me for my family name. When I proudly replied, "Matteï," she fell silent, and I could tell that this wasn't the right answer. Matteï had been my father's alias in the Resistance, and it stuck to him into the 1960s. So I was formally Hélène Miesseroff but often known as Lola Matteï.

This early confusion has luckily never caused me trouble with my identity. Further burdens were a twofold legacy of genocide, Jewish and Armenian, and a background that was Russophone, naturist, and libertarian—in other words, marginal with respect to almost all prevailing conventions.

I was going on seven when I asked my parents one day why they didn't wear wedding rings. "Because we're not married" was their reply. My prompt rejoinder to the effect that all parents were married took them by surprise, which shows how little control people have over the education of children once let loose in the wide world. When they did eventually marry, it was on the quiet, and to my great displeasure there was no ceremony. They merely went down, four of them, to the town hall, my parents on a motorbike and their two witnesses on a Vespa. At least there was chicken for lunch, a small luxury laid on as a thank-you to said witnesses.

A Peculiar Sex Education

We had no family in the region, and very little in the world at large. My parents said they did not regret this, and by far preferred our naturist "family of choice" to a biological family.

My mother and father met in Marseille just after the Second World War. My mother, who had been living in Paris, had fled there from the Nazis during the war, clandestinely crossing the demarcation line between the occupied zone and the free zone. My father had come to the city in search of sunshine after fighting with the Maquis in the Basses-Alpes department (now more grandly known as Alpes-de-Haute-Provence). Both had been born in Russia, and they soon discovered that they had both practiced nudism before the war—a remarkable coincidence, especially in those days. My father, then living in Lyon, would spend his holidays on the Île du Levant, which at the time was still entirely nudist, wild, and welcoming. My mother, in Paris, would spend her Sundays at the Physiopolis naturist center in Villennes-sur-Seine. Once settled in Marseille, they and a group of friends would go regularly, via the Calanque de Sugiton, to a big cove with fallen rocks where they could bathe naked. Something of a hike and a steep climb down were needed, and before long my mother, pregnant with me, was obliged to give this up. My father then dug out a little pond and set up

9

My parents and me at our Vieille-Chapelle naturist center, summer 1953

a volleyball court in the Vieille-Chapelle neighborhood, near his sandpaper factory, where friends could come and visit on weekends. This was the start of what was to become the first naturist colony in Marseille—the place where I grew up as part of the tribe of Free Culturists of Provence, or LCP, the name of our camp and a crude echo of the title of the German naturist federation the Freikörperkultur (FKK), or "Free Body Culture." For the sake of my family's good name, I must add that my parents and their friends were reviving a prewar association and, further, that my mother, an impeccable German speaker, having spent a good portion of her youth in Berlin, had no hand in this poor translation.

As much as its membership fluctuated, this tribe served well and truly as my family. When three of us, as children from the LCP, entered our first year in different classes at the nearby Lycée Marseilleveyre, we had no better way of explaining to our schoolmates what it was we had in common than the claim that we were cousins who spent our holidays together, likewise our Thursdays, Thursday being a home day at the time.

In our tribe there were adults of all kinds—of all genders, you might say—and consequently I formed no notion of "sexual orientation." Apart from traditional couples and families, there were female couples, male couples, and individuals of both sexes with a taste, or not, for their own counterparts. Some men were effeminate and some women were very butch. The term *homosexual* was unknown to me, and I had certainly never heard of queers or dykes, and for the longest time I had no idea how unusual the little world around me was.

And then there were some who managed to muddy the waters even more. Some women with female lovers might also have a man in their lives, and the same sort of thing went for some men. Vicky was the lover of Elula, a beautiful Eurasian with a long braid on one side and the future manager of the Katmandou and other gay clubs in Paris. I was still very small the day Vicky took me with her to say a long-distance hello to her boyfriend, who was locked up in the Baumettes prison. From street level I could hardly see her Pierrot, but that day, facing those high walls with their tiny windows, I conceived a hatred for all prisons. I also learnt that being Elula's lover in no way prevented her from loving a man for whom a wave from an unknown little girl was expected to provide comfort.

Tall Hélène, a nurse, was in love with little Françoise and was always calling her "sweetheart" or "darling." But Hélène also had a man in her life who was married with children. My mother told me later that their love story lasted a very long time but that Hélène wouldn't let the man leave his wife because of their children; Hélène herself had been made sterile by a mishandled catheter during an abortion. In those days vacuum aspiration did not yet exist; instead, a urinary catheter was used to provoke an inflammation that terminated the pregnancy—unless of course you resorted to a knitting needle or a parsley stalk. Later on, you were usually entitled to an in-hospital dilatation and curettage, accompanied by insults from the medical team. Fortunately for me, I never needed an abortion, whether by means of a catheter or by means of the Karman "super-coil" technique, much less by means of a parsley stalk!

Abortions were illegal in the 1950s, and my mother, who had seven before my birth, frequently, with my father's assistance, helped other women get one. Naturally I knew none of the details of these abortions, but I was soon involved, in that some of the women lodged with us and others left their children in our care. At least twice, Spanish women stayed with us for several days; in General Franco's very Catholic Spain, the repression was even worse than in France.

As for medical contraception, it was unknown. The Ogino (rhythm) method, based on the avoidance of sex during a woman's fertile time, and the only kind of birth control permitted by the Catholic Church, actually gave rise to a flood of babies. My mother had her German girlfriends smuggle in boxes of diaphragms (soon to be supplanted in France by cervical caps). With the advent of birth-control pills, I was immediately supplied with them, as were my friends.

The relationships of the men in our colony were no less complicated than the women's. Sylvain, for instance, was married to a charming woman whom, so osmotic was their relationship, we nicknamed "Sylvette." And they had a little girl. But I could clearly see that Sylvain was strongly attached to Charles. Meanwhile Bernard, who supposedly loved only men, suddenly became infatuated with a properly married Austrian woman some ten years his senior. All this was part of my everyday life and seemed perfectly normal.

The first time, it seems to me, that I became aware of the social repudiation of homosexuality was when I heard the story of Renée. A working-class girl, she was an apprentice hairdresser in Draguignan when she found herself in love with her female boss. She did not understand what was happening to her and suffered agonies over feelings that shame forbade her to reveal to anyone. Her distress came to an end when she encountered a local anarchist group whose members managed to rid her of her inhibitions. I wonder how she found the courage to tell them. I have to suppose that these comrades, noting her mannishness and sensing her discomfort, gave her a hand. The group promoted and practiced naturism and took a dim view of monogamy and the family, in the tradition of E. Armand (born Ernest-Lucien Juin), author notably of *La Révolution sexuelle et la camaraderie amoureuse* (Sexual revolution and amorous comradeship, 1934). Renée had to experience "amorous comradeship" for herself—with males too. I don't know what she thought about that, but she remained no less an anarchist and presumably no less a lesbian. She used to claim that if you want to know what you like, you have to try everything.

Did such a childhood necessarily seal my fate as a "fag hag"? That is far from certain. But it could hardly have readied me for the normal and normative life of a well-behaved young woman destined to become a proper mother of children.

At any rate, my marginal upbringing spared me a good many of the constraints that smothered French youth in the 1960s, and indeed the whole of French society as the so-called *Trente Glorieuses*—the thirty years from 1945 to 1975—ran their course. Sex was virtually taboo then, while my parents were singing odes to free love and all its delights. So effectively did they do so, in fact, that one fine day I was caught explaining to my little pals that female pleasure was not always part of the picture when you made love, and that guys should attend to this instead of leaping on women like louts. I was twelve and really didn't know what I was talking about; it was all theory, and vague theory at that. But I succeeded in impressing not just my pals but also the grown-up who overheard my disquisition by pure chance. I must admit, however, that the cult of sexual pleasure was not entirely positive for me. Paralyzed in a way by a parental superego, by its injunction to taste the joys of the flesh, I wasted a ridiculously long time before sloughing off my virginity. This delay was reinforced by older friends telling me how "the first time is really important." The upshot was that instead of letting myself go, I was forever wondering whether what I was doing with my boyfriend of the moment met the very high bar I had set. It is not hard to picture the effect on a pair of still-awkward kids.

Lessons in Rebellion

My parents, who never had any, held money in the greatest contempt. I was still very little when the sheds housing my father's workshops were destroyed by an accidental fire. Naturally there was no insurance. My father went to work as an electrical fitter and put in extra hours for years to pay off his suppliers. But it never even occurred to him to pay the business's income and social security taxes. The taxman made inquiries in the vicinity, and our neighbors declared unanimously that we were obviously penniless and unlikely to have squirreled away any money at all. One woman went so far as to tell the collector, "Those people are crazy. They have no money. They don't even have electricity. They have a little girl, and every night they sing, dance, and drink tea!" It was true, we were completely broke, but it didn't stop us making merry. My father would sit down at the piano or pick up his guitar and sing anything from Brassens to Russian Gypsy music. Everyone joined in, and those with any talent for playing, singing, or dancing happily participated.

So careless were my parents about money that they were capable of lending out sums they had just borrowed themselves, thus complying with—indeed outdoing—the Russian proverb that deems it "better to have a hundred friends than a hundred rubles." And sure enough, whenever it was time for me to leave for school, they would be reduced to rooting through pockets, bags, and all those nooks and crannies where coins can wind up, in search of the wherewithal for my bus fare and cafeteria lunch.

I must say I never heard my parents utter a word in favor of wage labor. They themselves embraced it as little as possible and held in the greatest esteem those who scorned it. At the LCP, the finest incarnation of the refusal of work was Henri Campagnol. He had a job with the City of Marseille Transport Authority (RATVM). He was on the lowest rung of the ladder as a cleaner of buses, trolley-buses and trams, and he strove to stay there: every time he was offered a promotion, he answered, much like Bartleby in Melville's eponymous story, that he would rather not accept. All his energy and ingenuity was devoted to working as little as possible. Consequently he became a sort of all-round champion of sick days and work injuries, and, as limited as this claim to fame was, it even spread abroad thanks to the naturists from all over, and especially from northern Europe, who came to stay with us. They would find Henri among us at our center every year, because he was almost always off work sick. They became aware of his ploys as soon as they asked him, in view of his manifestly radiant health, what particular malady he could be suffering from, after which they suggested others that he might be able to claim. So Henri's reputation as champion of not working soon resonated internationally. And guess what happened to him: to celebrate thirty-five years of fine loyal service, the RATVM presented Henri with their Worker's Medal of Honor!

With such models so close to home, it's no wonder that, come May 1968, I instantly embraced such slogans as "Never Work!" When my mother told a woman friend of hers how worried she was about my emphatic rejection of wage labor, the friend, a rock-ribbed anarchist, answered ironically: "Just tell me when Alyosha and you ever inculcated in your daughter the slightest sense of the nobility and value of work? When did you ever set her an example of a life devoted to toil?" That gave my mother pause, and she stopped worrying.

I also benefited, albeit unintentionally, from what might be called a political education. My mother was a White Russian, though this hardly mattered, for she was only four years old in 1917. As for my father, he had left the USSR at eighteen, in 1925. What this meant was that neither Marx nor Engels had a place in the vast family library; on the other hand, Voline, Kravchenko, Koestler and a good many other authors critical of the Soviet system were much in evidence, along with piles of anarchist books and pamphlets.

And then there were my father's recollections of the Resistance, which he later turned into a memoir of the Barrême Maquis, an iconoclastic little book, bitingly humorous, in which he recounts his own day-to-day experiences but excoriates mendacious ex post facto self-glorification of the Resistance, which he dubs "*le bidonus*"—i.e., a crock of shit.*

For her part, my mother regaled us endlessly with stories of the demonstrations during the Popular Front and the strike of 1936. She had been a typist at Citroën and, as she told it, the plant, occupied at the time, was a scene of nonstop festivity. There was dancing and music; she was twenty-three and had lots of student and artist

---

* First published as *Le Charme discret du maquis de Barrême* (1978); second edition: *Au maquis de Barrême: Souvenirs en vrac* (Marseille: Égrégores Éditions, 2006).

friends who came to join the assemblies as well as the celebration. A far cry from what we were to encounter in factories in May 1968.

The war in Algeria fueled passionate discussions among us; my parents circulated such banned books as Henri Alleg's *La Question*, which denounced torture by the French forces. I made the mistake of reading it when I was only eleven, and it gave me nightmares for years.

Arguments between the many anarchists and the few sorry members of the Communist Party rounded out the backdrop of my budding rebelliousness.

But I had yet to encounter class hatred.

After a long eviction court case, we were obliged to leave the rented property where we had been living in the Vieille-Chapelle district of Marseille. With encroaching urbanization, the Italian truck farmers around us and our own little paradise were no match for the frenzied development of the 1960s. My father found another lot for rent in the flatlands between Aubagne and Gémenos, and there we set about rebuilding sheds, digging out a swimming pool, planting trees and resuming our life without electricity and with water drawn from a well.

By this time I was in my second year of junior high, which meant that I now had a very long trip to school every day—two buses and a train—to get to Lycée Marseilleveyre, which was very close to our old center. Standing amid pine trees, with magnificent playing fields, Marseilleveyre was an experimental high school whose teaching methods and numerous other features were very much to my liking. But the travel was exhausting, and when I reached my last junior high year I resigned myself to transferring to a recently built lycée on the eastern outskirts of the city that was to be named after the writer and filmmaker

Marcel Pagnol. To get there, I first took a city bus as before (though one that came a little later), and then another bus, a school bus. It was in this second bus that two witches, girls from petty bourgeois shopkeeper families, began picking on Marinette, a shy girl whose parents were Spanish émigrés and sold clothes from a market stall—naturally an excellent reason for bullying her. I leapt to her defense, and war was declared. Marinette, who in fact soon learnt to defend herself, found out that the grandfather of one of her tormentors, an Italian immigrant at the beginning of the century, had started out selling socks from a pushcart. The pair were laughed off the stage. The following year, though, it was Rose they went after. Rose was not only "a fat and vulgar dirty blonde," she also had parents with a fairground shooting gallery. I didn't hesitate to tell her two persecutors where they got off, and I soon became friends with Rose, which allowed me, by the bye, to learn how to shoot.

Now that I had been introduced to the venom of the petty bourgeoisie, that of the big bourgeoisie would soon be painfully unveiled to me. First of all, the school saw an influx of pupils expelled from Lycée Périer, an incubator for those offspring of high Marseille society not entrusted to priests or nuns. This was how Anne landed in my class. Her father was the big boss of a public works contractor and the owner of a lovely farmhouse in a beautiful Haute-Provence village, of which he would later become mayor. He had a limousine driven by a chauffeur who often came to pick Anne up after school. This little rich girl carried a Hermès handbag and wore a fur-lined coat. But she was funny, cultured, smart, generous, and, I have to say it, very pretty. Between the two of us, strange to say, it was love at first sight. I soon told her who I was, where I lived, who my parents were—in fact, everything I had been scrupulously keeping from my classmates ever since I'd started high school. She came home with me, oohed and aahed at our wooden shack and the makeshift structures of the naturist center, pronounced our swimming pool magnificent, and adored my parents. And I went to her place, a very chic apartment in the very chic Prado neighborhood, and met her parents, who clearly took to me. Knowing how impecunious I was, Anne was subtle enough to sell me whatever records, accessories, and fine clothes I fancied at a low price, something that I failed to appreciate at the time because my notion of money was so vague. Only much later did I realize the great sensitivity she had shown: had she just given me these things, it would have seemed like charity, but by selling me them for a song, she let me think I was simply getting good deals.

But of course there had to be a snag. Being from the Marseille bourgeoisie, Anne was associated with three other rich kids expelled along with her from Lycée Périer and now at Marcel-Pagnol, though not in the same class as us. These three boys detested me. I was a foreigner, not very pretty, poorly turned out, with a big mouth but a reputation as brilliant and cultivated, and I had the respect not only of other students but also of teachers and administrators, whose authority I nevertheless continually challenged. None of which was a big deal, because I could hardly fail to shine in such a dismal setting, where I was like the proverbial one-eyed man in the country of the blind. This all made me especially loathsome in the eyes of those gilded dunces who, unable to attack me directly for fear of falling out with Anne, resorted to dirty tricks and humiliating remarks. They would ask me, for instance, where I was going skiing next season, as if my parents could possibly afford to send me to winter sports. Or they would compliment me condescendingly on some pathetic article of clothing, even going so far as to ironize over my supposed "culture" by saying how prodigious it was that a girl like me could write a paper on existentialism or be so well acquainted with the classics, and claiming that this must be attributable to my White Russian roots. And even though I stood up to their taunting and openly poured scorn on them, I was still left seething inside.

About that time, our lycée took in a group of kids repatriated from Algeria. Some of these "*pieds-noirs*" became fast friends of mine; others were extreme rightists and worshipped the OAS, the Secret Army Organization, whose operations continued until almost 1965. Relations with these newcomers were more than tense, even violent, despite the fact that "politics" was officially banned on school property. Pamphlets and newspapers were strictly forbidden, and once even my copy of the national news-weekly *Le Nouvel Observateur*, then supposedly left-wing, was confiscated from me.

In the 1960s, French schools and workplaces were even more ossified by hierarchical and normative structures than they are today, and things were naturally even more rigid for women. Right up until 1965, a wife needed the official authorization of her husband to take a job or open a bank account. The girls in my school were not allowed to wear pants and were forced to don a beige smock that was not imposed on the boys.

Sex was repressed, and precocious girls lived in continual fear of getting pregnant; rape was never spoken of, and homosexuality barely more. For my part I vigorously supported freedom for women, abortion and homosexuality, and somewhat naïvely I convinced myself

I was a pacifist so that I could protest against the war and against the conscription that awaited the guys. But I came from another world, and this was so glaringly obvious that I made a secret of my naturist life, telling only my closest friends about it. All the same, like the others, I was confined by the straitjacket against which the young all over the world were starting to chafe.

Wherein I Am Dubbed "Fag Hag"

I arrived in Aix-en-Provence in the fall of 1965 as a new student in the university's humanities department. My friend Alban, who used to come with his mother to our naturist center, had already been in Aix for three years, and he was like a big brother to me. Alban got me used to reading *Le Monde* every day; I did not yet think of it as the "official record of all powers that be," as the Situationists would scathingly call it. He steered me to Jean Genet, Julien Gracq, and a good many other authors. And he taught me to drink tea without sugar. He escorted me to ballets at the Opéra de Marseille, where he was comped for having provided the choreographer Joseph Lazzini with the theme for his *Revolving Door*. Alban was like a romantic leading man, dark, tall and slim, with almond eyes and a sensual mouth. He was also homosexual, which prevented me from falling in love with him. And which likely led to our remaining close until his cruel death in 1972 in a car accident, a death I have never really gotten over.

So Alban was my mentor during my time in Aix. The day I arrived, he took me for lunch at the student restaurant, where I received a welcome worthy of a debutante from a would-be Proustian coterie that immediately adopted me. Members included François and his lover Lucie, blonde with dark eyes and very much a *woman*, both from Salon-de-Provence; Virginie, a little redhead, chubby and sweet;

Alban

and Blanche, a tall brunette whose jade eyes gleamed with mordant irony. Blanche once proclaimed, after having made love for the first time, that "All in all, it's no better than coffee," and she urged us, given the way the world was going, to call 1966 "the year of buffoonery." She was from Avignon, where her parents had a store and her older brother ran an antique shop with his male companion.

And then there was Jimmy, a cute, brilliant little Eyetalian brimming with talent and vitality, and incidentally an ephebophile. He was unquestionably the prime mover of this little group. Jimmy was the one who held us together, the one who oversaw the ritual selection of whomever of whatever sex in the queue at the student restaurant (which we continued to frequent) was to be invited to join our table for a droll parody of an elegant lunch party.

In a literature class, I met Michel, the one and only friend I ever made on the benches of a university that it wouldn't take me long to leave. Michel was a pork butcher's son and a great lover of baroque music, a lonely and tormented guy. Jimmy, a great one for inventing nicknames, called him "Michel the Sad." Unlike me, Michel was attracted by muscular men. Convinced, however, that my distaste was just an act, he called me his "Pentelic liar," explaining, because I did not understand, that Pentelic marble was the white stone used for Greek statues and the Parthenon's masonry. Later he allowed as how I was not really made of stone. I was hardly surprised when Michel made a conquest in the shape of Léo, a tall, dark and handsome male of Greek extraction, and the pair became lovers. We enjoyed playing the trio, after the fashion of *Jules and Jim*, although I slept with neither of them, nor with anyone else for that matter.

One day Michel stunned me with this peremptory judgment: "Some girls love sailors, some love soldiers, but you, my dear, are a real fag hag!" I was eighteen and not ready to be pigeonholed like that. Some time later my father, who didn't know a thing about saints, added his two cents: "In the church they have their Rita, Saint of Whores; in our house we have Lola, Saint of Fags." Even though both sainthood and prostitution were closed books to me, I had to admit that I must indeed be a "fag hag."

It was true enough that whenever I became friends with a boy there was a good chance he would be homosexual; I seemed to be a magnet to men-loving men. For instance, when I went with Michel, Alban, and two other male friends to an off-season Île du Levant, the place was not crowded. The guys went off happily to cruise the island but returned empty-handed only to find me surrounded by three young men who manifestly had no designs on my virtue. Shortly afterwards, when Alban ran into me at the faculty cafeteria in the company of two markedly effeminate newcomers, he reiterated that I was most definitely a "fag catcher." I saw no reason to take offense: after all, the Native Americans had their "dream catchers."

I doubt I could be called a fag catcher today, for now *pédé* (fag) always seems to serve as an insult. At the time, however, the term was neutral, because *homosexual*, still less than a hundred years old, was marred by its unwelcome medical or legal connotation of "socialized sexual deviance" (Guy Hocquenghem). Homosexuality was still viewed as a "social plague," and one had to read Raymond Queneau to come across a benevolent reference like Zazie's charming talk of "homorsessuals." *Invert*, *sodomite*, and *homoerotic* were distinctly outdated. Women could be referred to politely as *lesbiennes* rather than *gouines* (dykes), but for guys *pédés* was really the only choice. The gay review *Arcadie* had sought to promote the term *homophile*, but without much success. In a pinch you could say someone was "that way," so avoiding the noxious "one of those."

It was not long before I became part of a small Aix demimonde rife with *pédés* and *gouines*. We frequented the Café des Deux Garçons—the "Two Gs" to us—where artists and bourgeois rubbed shoulders with impoverished students, apprentice hairdressers, store owners, and waiters. A fancy Afghan hound named Zeus used to come in with a couple of lady antique dealers, while a young worker might occasionally be seen being chatted up by the scion of a banking dynasty. As for our group, we discovered we had no less than three shopkeepers' children among us. In short, the place was a great social melting pot made possible by modest prices that clashed with the luxurious but faded decor of this historic brasserie. Every evening we settled down in the place's barroom, which was presided over by a much-made-up and bejeweled old cashier whom Jimmy nicknamed "Castafiore," after Hergé's diva.

Before long I was introduced to the great lyrical voices to be heard at the Opéra de Marseille, and then, the following summer, at the Chorégies d'Orange festival. But the Aix festival was not for me. Too pricey, too posh, too bourgeois. For Jimmy and me, the best annual event was unquestionably Barbara's concert tour. As yet, among other gay icons, Dalida was no more than a singer with a foreign accent and Mylène Farmer was just a little girl, so Barbara was our idol. We would go to her dressing room after the show, each bearing a long-stemmed red rose to present her with. We left overwhelmed by the warm greeting and few kind words she bestowed on us.

During that first winter in Aix, I started to develop a personal style. Unable to afford fashionable clothes, I outfitted myself at Emmaus thrift stores with the sort of things that would be called "vintage" nowadays—a notion quite unheard of at the time. I took to wearing big hats, long fishnet gloves and, when it was cold, a fur muff. To complete this offbeat look, I used a great deal of makeup

Me in 1969

for much-darkened eyes and a chalk-white complexion.
If in this I anticipated the goths yet to come, it was only
because I was penniless.

   We kept very much to ourselves for protection against
the bigotry and attacks directed at homosexuals. It has to
be said, though, that some of our gay guys liked living on

the edge. Cruising at Jourdan Park or other pickup spots put them in danger of being beaten up or ripped off by fakers, gay bashers, or the occasional repressed homosexual. Jimmy was regularly stalked by a creep who loved to frighten him. Which was easy enough, given that Jimmy was slight and his pursuer sturdy. Jimmy lived far from the center of town, and he would go home at night shit-scared. As for Alban, he showed up from time to time with a black eye, bruises or even worse. One night we had to take a friend to the hospital with a bad head wound. And then there were those who went in for brief encounters in public urinals, which they called *tasses*, or "cups." (This was before the Decaux coin-operated toilet booths came in.) So-called back rooms (the English word), dark places for anonymous sexual commerce, did not yet exist; there were bathhouses for sure, but not everywhere, and I suspect that the *tasses* were more exciting, more transgressive—and free to boot. One evening in Nîmes, I was supposed to meet Michel, who was downhearted after breaking up with Léo. I waited for him near the rail station by a urinal that he had suddenly chosen to visit in search of consolation and got to observe the motley fauna hanging around, along with the crusts of piss-soaked bread left by the *soupeurs* who got off by sucking on them. As dusk fell and the passersby seemed to me more and more shady, I got a sense of how dangerous it had to be for a young man venturing into a *tasse* in the dead of night.

My First Gang

I was always aware that, along with my male friends, I was in danger, especially after nightfall. The most effective way to counteract that danger, and the most agreeable, was to stay together, go around as a group, hold fear at bay, and reassure each other but always be ready to do battle. These were the survival tactics we developed in Aix in January 1967.

With Catherine, a sweet little blonde girl who masked her depth behind a wacky exterior and who was then my soul sister, I rented a two-room apartment in a street so narrow that its name was Rue Esquiche-Coude, or "Squish-Elbow Street," the verb *esquicher* being a local word. ("Northerners"—who begin for Marseille natives no farther north than Valence—would use *écraser*.) The place was soon flooded by a stream of young people, girls and boys, straight and gay or a bit of both. We spent long stretches of time together, particularly at night, changing the world by the light of votive candles gathered on expeditions to the city's many churches—which also furnished us with a variety of gold knickknacks and several prie-dieux that stood in for chairs. Oftentimes night morphed into day, and then we would stay where we were with the shutters closed. As Alban once said to my mother, "Génia, your daughter is out of her mind. I come to visit her at three in the afternoon and can't see a thing because the

30

shutters are closed and she is calling wildly for someone to go and get candles right away so they don't have to stay in the dark!" When it came to food and drink, we stole unrestrainedly. We drank quite a lot, some more than others, and there was never enough to slake every thirst. On days without anything, we would buy 90 percent medicinal alcohol from the pharmacy and mix it with Coke. This must have been the fashion, because, on a weekend visit to my parents, a friend of theirs, an eye doctor's nurse in a Marseille clinic, warned me that the consumption of methyl or wood alcohol was giving rise to vision problems among young people, leading in some cases to blindness. I realized then why my mother, who made cheap vodka using over-the-counter grain alcohol, was careful to tell the pharmacist what she wanted it for. I believe it is because of that time that methyl alcohol is now usually tinted so as to distinguish it from ethyl spirits.

We also tried our first joints in those days, and we were quite full of ourselves over it. I confess we had a little trouble inhaling with our earliest ones, rolled in newsprint cones by some English friends. I wasn't much smitten myself, but that was too bad, because I was duty bound to commune in this way with the Beat poets I so much admired. As yet we knew nothing of the euphoria induced by sniffing ether, freely available at the time—and as for so-called hard drugs, needles had not so much as pricked our universe.

Apart from Catherine and me, there were Gilles and Laurent, Corsicans and filmmakers-to-be. I first saw Gilles in a Marseille student hangout, dancing like a bear and wobbling his big head. His hair was all curls, he had a strong Corsican accent, and he charmed me at once. He seemed both very old and very young to me, different, mysterious, and somehow malign. To sound interesting, and since he hadn't told me his name, I claimed that he was a reincarnation of Gilles de Rais. When I ran into him on campus, disappointed to find out that he was just another dumb student, I introduced him to Catherine as Gilles. When we became friends, he remained Gilles for all of us, and even his pal Laurent, a brooding individual who soon joined our gang, tended to call him Gilles rather than Antoine, his actual name.

A trio of girls soon swelled our ranks. Of the three, Agnès was the most excitable. A petite brunette with big green eyes, a heavy drinker ready for anything, she was passionate and passably suicidal.

It was Agnès who brought us Élian from her philosophy class, another big drinker, quite crazy, who claimed to be queer and an Althusserian. The name of Althusser meant nothing to me, but when Élian went down the street shouting, "Marx, Engels, Lenin, Stalin, Mao!" it gave Catherine and me a jolting preview.

Coco, a svelte young man, rather effeminate with a pretty birdlike head, became one of ours and one of my closest friends. Coco knew every nook and cranny of Marseille's queer world.

Of course, we already had Alban, Jimmy and Michel, along with Magali, a friend from back at Lycée Marcel-Pagnol, and her companion, Marie-Claude; also Jean-Christophe, a dedicated mountain climber and another Pagnol alum; and the future film director Jean-Henri Roger.

We were hungry for new experiences, repelled and desperate in face of the petty bourgeois prospects on offer so long as we were good students. For my part, I had the utmost contempt for the university, for most of its teachers,

Jimmy and Magali performing at the naturist center of Les Joncquiers in 1967

and for its oh-so-obedient students. In March 1967, a rather unsympathetic article in *Le Nouvel Observateur* led me to the pamphlet *De la misère en milieu étudiant* (Of the poverty of student life), and I found that it echoed my own feelings perfectly.* I began to consider dropping out of a university that I already barely ever attended. Then I read issue 11 of the review *Internationale situationniste*, along with Raoul Vaneigem's *Traité de savoir-vivre à l'usage des jeunes générations* and Guy Debord's *La Société du spectacle*, both published in 1967.† These publications shaped my critical worldview, Catherine's also, and prepared us in the best possible way to embrace the portents of the May 1968 uprising. By contrast, Gilles, Jean-Christophe, and Jean-Henri made common cause with the Maoists—indeed with the most Stalinist faction of the Maoists. Gilles would go on to work for the review *Cinéthique*, aligned with the structuralo-Maoist *Tel Quel* tendency. Jean-Henri would join the Dziga Vertov Group, led by Godard and Jean-Pierre Gorin, and contribute to the production of inept militant films, pretentious and soporific; he made up for

---

* *De la misère en milieu étudiant: Considérée sous ses aspects économique, politique, psychologique, sexuel et notamment intellectuel, et de quelques moyens pour y remédier* (Strasbourg: Union Nationale des Etudiants de France, 1966). First English translation, adapted and expanded: *Ten Days That Shook the University: Of Student Poverty Considered in Its Economic, Political, Psychological, Sexual, and Particularly Intellectual Aspects, and a Modest Proposal for Its Remedy* (London: Situationist International, 1967); widely published thereafter in various versions as *On Student Poverty*. —Trans.

† English translations: Raoul Vaneigem, *The Revolution of Everyday Life*, rev. ed. (Oakland: PM Press, 2012) and Guy Debord, *The Society of the Spectacle* (New York: Zone, 1994), both trans. Donald Nicholson-Smith. See also Ken Knabb's annotated translation of Debord's *Society of the Spectacle* (Berkeley, CA: Bureau of Public Secrets, 2014).

this later with *Neige* (1981) and *Cap Canaille* (1983), both excellent movies that he directed with Juliet Berto.

But when we embarked on our collective adventure, all that was in the future. For the time being we were focused on attacking all social norms, this in a rather instinctive way and with the feeling that our fused relationships would confer a kind of immunity upon us. The neighbors threw stones through our windows, cut off our electricity and called the cops on us regularly, but we laughed it all off; every time we fled wildly after some burglary or dine-and-dash, we were thrilled, and our bonds grew stronger.

We provoked scandal almost anywhere and at every opportunity. We smooched with anyone, male or female, whom we fancied and jeered at anyone offended by it. Fashionable people, attracted by our beautiful youth and angry energy, would invite us to their soirées, where we would behave in the most outrageous possible ways. In the street we covered government buildings with graffiti. Agnès daubed red lipstick on the statues at the so-called Palais de Justice and for good measure scrawled words like "whore" and "idiot" on their brows. In a word, we outdid the rowdiest of rowdy students.

These flamboyant transgressions were accompanied by a sexual life far less unbridled than one might imagine or than we would have had people believe. The greater part of our affection went to the group we were forming, so much so, in fact, that, as Catherine used to say, "We make love in stacks, like sea hares"—but the love in question was well-nigh platonic, largely confined to kissing and petting.

There were of course love affairs within the group, between guys and between guys and girls—not so much between girls. But things did not always go swimmingly. Agnès had a crush on Élian but was resigned to her love going unrequited. On the other hand, she had a little scene with Jimmy, who was soft on her because she reminded him of the *Saint Sebastian* with imploring eyes and long hair of Il Sodoma, the Italian Renaissance painter with the unequivocal name. In the midst of a very well-lubricated night at the house of the heir to a large textile fortune, Agnès happened upon Élian and Jimmy in full amorous embrace. Her heart skipped a beat. She grabbed a guitar and used it as a bludgeon to lay about the two lads, screaming that she was going to kill them. By this time everyone was three sheets to the wind, but at first we did manage to restrain her. Then she found a bottle of Pour un Homme de Caron in the bathroom and took two good swigs. We had to cart her back to her studio apartment, but nobody noticed that she had put the bottle of cologne in her pocket. She made herself become violently ill and smashed the bottle on the parquet floor. Once her doubly broken heart had healed, she was obliged to stay away from her place for over a fortnight until the scent had dissipated and she could go in without vomiting.

We were continually insulted, called filthy fags or filthy lezzies, but we didn't take it lying down. Sometimes we even found unexpected allies, like the time some little fascist thugs tried to eject us violently from a bar. As we were resisting, Gilles called out in Corsican to Laurent to mind out, a guy was coming up behind him. At which two brawny characters sitting in the rear of the place, whom we would hardly have suspected of friendly feelings for us, sprang to their feet and shouted, likewise in Corsican, "Okay, that changes everything!" They had our back, and together we routed the aggressors.

We invented antimisogynous games. Sitting at a bar, a few girls, we would send a note to some young guy that appealed to us, inviting him over for a drink, and when he came we would subject him to a mocking inquisitorial barrage of questions. Those who went for this did not usually emerge unscathed, but a few passed the test with flying colors. We even made some new friends in this way. We also liked for a few of us to surround a guy in the street and provoke him: "Is all that really yours? You're really sexy, you know. You have a cute little ass, lovely eyes"— all the garbage that we were always being subjected to ourselves.

Realizing that our group was bound to break up eventually, we resolved on one drunken night, a fifteenth of April, that we would hold a reunion in Paris exactly ten years later. A perfectly trite idea—much later it was even the theme of a popular song.* Thanks to Agnès, who wrote the date down on her identity card so as not to forget it, and thanks also to the rather surprising fact that we remained more or less in contact over the years, nearly all of us did indeed get together on the evening of April 15, 1977, in Paris, not at Place des Grands Hommes, as per the title of the song, but rather under the Pont de l'Alma on the Left Bank. We didn't have much to say to one another: we had taken very different paths since May 1968. I tied one on, and although I can still call up Coco and I reviling procreation and family life, the rest is a blur. It was sad, and I wondered why the Corsicans decided that we should have a big commemorative do in 1987. That event, as it turned out, was a success: we pretended we still loved each other, but, at least for me, the heart was not in it. And when, still later, Gilles suggested renting a large house and

---

* "Place des Grands Hommes," written and sung by Patrick Bruel (1989). —Trans.

making a film about our exploits of yore, I refused point-blank, and the idea died the death.

Back then, though, there we were, hurling insults and charging nightly through the streets yelling revolutionary slogans, ever ready for the fray. There we were, a year in advance, on the doorstep of May '68.

Lavender Nights

In Marseille, Coco, Alban and Jimmy often took us to a gay club in the Opéra neighborhood run by one Madame Jackie Guérini, a member of the Mafia family then dominating the city. The club was called Le Paradou, but wisecracker Jimmy rebaptized it "Le Parachute." Our little clutch of five girls was welcome, but there was no question of our bringing others: this was a boys' club and was going to remain that way, as the boss lady stated in no uncertain terms. So when there were more of us, we had to go farther from the city center, to La Mare au Diable (The Devil's Pool), named for the George Sand novel, where there were plenty of women—which of course suited Magali and Marie-Claude just fine.

But Le Paradou was closer, and much more fun, especially since it was there that Lady Jane appeared most often and with the most flair. "La Jeanne," as she was familiarly called, was what was known as a burlesque transvestite; today she might be described as a drag artist. In private life Lady Jane was simply Jean, a stocky guy in nondescript clothes strolling with his brother and parents by the Old Port or spending Sunday with them at a *cabanon* by one of the *calanques* without his effeminate mannerisms ruffling the general tranquility.* Onstage, however, Lady

---

* *Calanques* are narrow, steep-walled coves typical of the Mediterranean coast of southern France. *Cabanons* in this context are former fishermen's

Jane was terrific, by turns La Traviata, La Tosca, La Piaf, La Mistinguett, and even Cleopatra with a plastic snake slithering across her chest—all elaborate, far-out turns, wildly comical, and far outstripping all the competition. Transvestites performed in nearly all the gay joints I got to know, but La Jeanne was possessed of an intelligence, a culture and a humor that I had rarely encountered. She was my heroine, and I loved everything about her, even the cocktail she invented: vodka-grapefruit-grenadine, aka the Lady Jane. This became my favorite drink in May 1968 thanks to the bartender at the café where the Aubagne Action Committee used to meet, and to which he and I both belonged.

When I went up to Paris, I often hooked up with Fabrice, a former lover of Jimmy's who was studying modern dance and about to embark on a distinguished career. We would go to bars and clubs in Saint-Germain-des-Prés like Le Nuage, Le Cherry Lane or Le Fiacre. There was also Le Pousse-au-Crime, a lesbian bar, and La Mendigote, a restaurant near the Hôtel de Ville. When we finished our crawl, or if we were out of funds, we all went to Fabrice's place, a small studio apartment on Rue Saint-André-des-Arts. His upstairs neighbor was none other than the Letterist Isidore Isou. We really were young fools: when Isou came down to complain about the noise, we thought it was cute to respond with onomatopoeic pastiches of Letterist poetry.

In Aix we regularly patronized Le Dinosaure, a joint with hardly any customers. The boss, who may have thought we would get him out of the doldrums, gave us

---

shacks overlooking the water, now often owned by local families who visit them on weekends to bathe, picnic and play pétanque. —Trans.

Lady Jane

a warm welcome and frequently offered us free rounds.
He did not seem to be gay, but he left us completely free
to do whatever we wanted. As a way of thanking him, I
suggested to my friends that we could get his place some
publicity by organizing a party there, and everyone agreed.

As it turned out, however, it fell to me alone to talk to him about the arrangements, at which he decided, assuming that I enjoyed some kind of notoriety or some kind of experience in such matters, that it would be *my* event. Without consulting me, he had invitations printed up for a "Lola Soirée," which embarrassed me no end. La Jeanne agreed to come and do her number, and the whole gang sent out invites. From the start we decided that it would be a private affair—something unheard of short of renting a function room. As in all places frequented by homosexuals, arrivals needed to be screened, and for that job we hired Georgie, a solid and sly little Armenian who looked like a hoodlum. The evening was a rousing success: the place was chock full, and friends had come from all over, many in outrageous garb. We were treated to a trio from the Côte d'Azur—Julien, his male lover, and his wife—all dressed in white; a captivating *métis* sporting a belt of bananas in the manner of Josephine Baker slung around skin-tight gold lamé pants; boy-girls in smoking jackets; girlfriends of both sexes in ball gowns; and a host of other splendors. The mood was friendly, tender, warm, and overwhelmingly joyful. About five in the morning, the boss came over to congratulate me and hand me an envelope stuffed with bills that he said represented my commission. I categorically refused to profit off my friends that way, but he forced me to take the money. I don't know how much was in the envelope, but it was enough to cover food and drink at La Rotonde, which stayed open all night, for all those still standing.

Later, the boss convinced me to arrange a repeat performance. Success was obviously guaranteed; people were soon fighting for invitations. A friend whose parents kept a store in Aix found his younger brother dolling himself up in great agitation and asked where he was off to that made him go to such lengths. To which the young man replied that he had managed to get invited to a soirée put on by a big star of the town's nighttime scene. Imagine his disappointment when his brother told him that he was a dope, because the so-called big star was none other than his good friend Lola, whom he had met many a time.

By chance this second soirée afforded me an opportunity to indulge in a pleasurable petty act of revenge. Georgie called me over, as he always did when uninvited guests showed up at the door claiming to know me. To my great surprise I found myself face to face with those three rotten bourgeois guys from the lycée, and to my great satisfaction I was able to tell them that yes, we had had gone to the same school, that yes, I knew them only too well, but that no, we had never been friends, and to conclude by signaling to a grinning Georgie that he should get rid of "this trash" forthwith. It was a sight for sore eyes to see their reactions and their humiliating retreat before the muscled insistence of little Georgie, who, though quite ignorant of the circumstances, had instantly got the memo.

That evening affair, or more precisely the evening before it, foreshadowed a turning point that would soon change the whole course of my life. I was alone at Le Dino making final arrangements for the second "Lola Soirée" when all of a sudden who should walk in but Léo Ferré. I thought I was dreaming. He sat down at a table with Marie-Christine Diaz, then his new young lover, later his wife, while his enormous dog quenched its thirst at a champagne bucket. I have never understood how come they wound up there. They invited me to join them; this was early May, they had just arrived from Paris, and Ferré told me about the unfolding events in characteristically poetic, epic, and exhilarating terms: uprising, barricades, cobblestones, tear gas, riots in the streets... With my head already filled as it was with Situationist ideas, I found all this far more exciting than what the radio had been telling me. And a thousand times more exciting than our pathetic little demonstration in February against the removal of Henri Langlois from the directorship of the Cinémathèque Française, of which he was one of the founders. We had gone to protest, not very effectively, at movie theaters patronized by crowds of students who hadn't the faintest idea that Langlois was a great pioneer of film history and film preservation.

When Léo and Marie-Christine agreed to come to my event the next day, I didn't really believe them, but sure enough they joined us. Not for long, admittedly, because a transvestite, a great fan of Ferré's, pounced on the singer and tried to cover him with kisses. Only with great difficulty did we manage to drag him away. This incident added not a little spice to a soirée already far more boisterous than its predecessor.

A few days later, Le Dino's owner informed me that he was in talks with people about buying a club where I could organize more soirées beginning that summer, and that in a few months, when I reached my majority (twenty-one in those days), I could become the place's manager. I thanked him nicely and made my exit from his world, in which I already sensed I could never play a part. The May '68 movement was astir now for us too, and this put paid not only to the besequined role I was being groomed for but also to the cohesion of our Aix squad.

This brief period of nightclubbing (to use an Anglicism popularized in the 1970s by the punk dandy Alain Pacadis as a columnist in the daily paper *Libération*) would nevertheless enjoy an amusing revival for me that August, when

I never had a nightclub career, but in 1992 I starred in a video for the alternative rock group Les Garçons Bouchers (The Butcher Boys).

I was working as a traveling product promoter in supermarkets in the South of France. My circuit brought me to a small town on the coast where a friend of mine was a reporter for a regional newspaper. For a laugh he placed an announcement in the local-news section of his rag to the effect that "the Régine of Aix-en-Provence" was to honor the city with her presence, that she was a Russian princess who as always would be accompanied by superb young men, that she would be arrayed in fabulous costumes, and a load of other such blarney. His boss asked him for an introduction to me, and the rival paper, loath to miss the train, echoed the item and added blather of its own. All this for a twenty-year-old girl hawking cordials and pastis in the food-and-drink aisles of a supermarket! What it taught me, at any rate, long before reality TV, was that stardom can be constructed from next to nothing.

Gigolos and Gigolettes

In that world of bars and nightclubs, prostitution was always more or less present, even if you needed sharp eyes to detect it. In those days, my own eyes were at least half-open.

At about fourteen, in Aubagne, I began hanging out with the kids in "*le Cours*" (pronounced with a hissing final *s*), meaning the Cours Jean-Jaurès, the town's main square. They included a clique referred to as *blousons noirs*, although they would more accurately have been described as blue-jean jackets, because very few could manage to buy—and much less steal—the proverbial black leather ones. It was among them that I first ran into what would later be called homophobia, and it got under my skin: they called me crazy because, apart from reading books, itself clearly deviant, I stood up for "lezzies and fags." Oddly enough, nobody took exception to the distinctly effeminate mannerisms of Diego, a young Rom I was fond of. But Diego was "family," belonging as he did to a clan of Spanish Gitanos who had settled locally and whose sons, as soon as they reached fifteen, automatically joined this gang of young loafers, the *vitelloni* of the place. My mother, always well informed by her friend the gay waiter at the Grand Café du Commerce, told me that Diego rented himself out to the foreign legionnaires who had been garrisoned in the town since the end of the Algerian war. I must admit that this rather shocked me.

At my lycée I "dated" a mixed-race boy who was hand-some, elegant, sensitive, and considerate. The kids from Aubagne said he was a snob—"snobs" being the adversaries of the *blousons noirs* rather as mods were the opponents of rockers in England. One day he told me about a club near Toulon where he went occasionally with pals of his. Long afterwards, putting two and two together, I realized that he must have been meeting older men there; his large working-class family could never have afforded the fancy clothes he wore.

In Aubagne I quite soon forsook the kids on the Cours for Kim—the daughter of a German legionnaire and a Vietnamese woman who ran a restaurant with "hostesses," also known as *serveuses-montantes* (waitresses who "went upstairs")—and Jean-Michel, a veteran of the little band of teenagers with whom I used to take the train when I was at Lycée Marseilleveyre. At that time I still didn't know, and probably nor did he, that Jean-Michel liked boys. Now he introduced André to us, a very feminine and very funny guy, the first genuine queen I ever met in my life. We used to stroll through the little town, the four of us, scathingly decrying its ugliness and mediocrity.

Kim seemed more well heeled than the rest of us; her mother, after all, was a businesswoman. She would give us little gifts, and we thought nothing of it until the day we learnt she had been busted for shoplifting and charged with numerous petty larcenies. She was only fifteen, but in view of her "family environment" she was confined to Bon-Pasteur, a horrific reformatory run by nuns. Once we went to see her, stationing ourselves along the route taken by the file of girl "wards of justice" on their weekly outing with their cornet-wearing minders. Kim seemed so distressed when she saw us that we never went again. I ran into her some years later, hustling at a Marseille bar in the Opéra district, and then again amid the streetwalkers on Rue Saint-Denis in Paris, where I stupidly asked what she was doing there. On both occasions she acted so embarrassed that I let her be.

One day in the late 1960s, as I was walking past the entrance to a hotel, not far from the Opéra de Marseille, where a few whores liked to hang, I heard my name called. I turned and found myself face to face with a tall brunette who then removed her wig and said: "Come on, Lola, don't you recognize me? It's André, your old pal from Aubagne." André was hooking in drag, he told me, because his clients were more comfortable going upstairs with a girl. That made two from my old quartet who had ended up on the game. I long drew comfort from the notion that this had been a free choice on their part, but in reality their main motive was no doubt to avoid the shop floor.

The beginning of the 1967 school year in Aix saw our circle widen. Among the new recruits were several handsome local high schoolers brought in by Jimmy, while Coco introduced a clone of the young Darío Moreno, a Tahitian queen with big velvety eyes, solidly built and cuddly. Jimmy's cute boys made me their confidante, their big sister, their beard, introduced me to their mothers, picked out the clothes I should wear, and kept a jealous eye on me by fending off as best they could any suitors I happened to attract. But they succumbed to the allure of Teddy, a nice-looking little delinquent from Paris who unfortunately fell in love with me. I flirted with him, let him sleep in my bed, allowed him a few liberties, and I showed him off like a trophy, even had him dance on a coffee table for my girlfriends. He was a pusher, and I would find lumps of hash in the silverware drawer, amid my underwear, or in other unlikely hiding places. He was also something of a thief and was always bringing me gifts, jewelry, clothes, things stolen from women or men to whom he had granted sexual favors. Now and again people would ask me whether I had happened to find some necklace, vase, or cashmere scarf around my place—items I hastened to return. When I was questioned about a TV, however, I pled not guilty to the charge of receiving stolen property. Teddy claimed to be a gigolo, and taking him at his word, I sent him off to hire himself out to an old Marseille lawyer I knew. I can't say I was completely at ease about this at the time, and I fancy the same might be said of him, because he immediately blew the money the assignation had earned him by buying me a magnificent powder compact and taking me out to a posh restaurant. This, my one and only venture into proxenetism, led me to break off quickly with Teddy, and it remains one of my most shameful memories. When I gave Teddy his marching orders, he turned nasty, screaming, throwing kitchen knives at the panic-stricken twinks, and spending the night on my doormat before giving up and leaving Aix altogether.

Coco was fascinated by the gigolos at Le Paradou. He even tried his own hand at it, which was a fiasco. His pseudo-customer, barely older than us, decided to play along only because he had instantly realized that Coco was no more a real gigolo than he himself was a real john. Once at the hotel, Coco could no longer keep up the act, and all the pair could do was talk and laugh, which they were still doing when they rejoined us and told us the story.

Others were more gifted. One day I asked one of them how he managed to get a hard-on with all the decrepit twink-seeking old guys who were his stock-in-trade. His reply was, "Crinkle a big bill by my ear and you'll see!"

I had a few girlfriends who were hookers, again in the vicinity of the Opéra de Marseille. They were from poor and often oppressive families. One of them, Houria, had originally had the very worst of jobs—a job once used to threaten underperforming schoolgirls: "If you don't improve, you'll end up on the dates." In other words, standing all day packing dates into boxes with her bare hands. When, on top of that, Houria's parents decided to marry her off, she ran away and fell into the clutches of a pimp who, luckily for her, was quite soon murdered. She managed to remain independent after that, preferring prostitution, so she told me, to the life that had been laid out for her. But I saw many others fall prey to the heroin that helped them carry on and—in the words of Houria, who flirted with the drug—"escape a little from this shitty life."

I was stunned, on the other hand, by the young bourgeois girls who turned tricks just so they could buy fancy clothes. At the Triboulet, a bar in Rue Haxo, you would see them toting the fashion magazine *Elle* around and pointing out the suit or dress they fancied to the *patronne*. They needed to find a sugar daddy ASAP. Indeed, when *Elle* ran a feature on the most fashionable young ladies of France's provincial cities, the Marseille pick turned out to be one of the sugar babies well known to me. Of course, all of these girls were destined to straighten up and make good marriages. Meanwhile, however, the word was that the uptick in venereal disease among the trendy young guys who patronized Pierre, a bar across the street from the police station, could be laid at their feet.

It has to be said that in those days prostitution was everywhere in Marseille. Gigolos and transvestites were ever present in Rue Curiol, the most impoverished girls were in Rue Thubaneau, the youngest and prettiest around the Opéra and Avenue du Prado, while the most elegant professionals worked Brasserie Le Cintra on the port, where I long mistook them for idle rich ladies. And these were just the neighborhoods where I went myself; Marseille was still a real port, and there were plenty of sailors' dives in La Joliette and beyond.

Whenever we went out at night, we were bound to be solicited. But aside from Coco's abortive experiment, none of us was ever tempted more than fleetingly by the prospect of drinking champagne on the deck of a yacht or leaving for a weekend in Venice, possibly as a group, with the gentlemen who so kindly offered us such thrills.

The last time I might have been tempted myself was in an after-hours place in Paris when I was well past thirty. There was a regular there, not really beautiful but very seductive, who escorted moneyed foreigners to museums, concerts, theaters, and expensive restaurants. For this you needed, like her, to be cultured, polyglot, well turned out, and well versed in gastronomy and enology. But, or so she claimed, you didn't necessarily have to sleep with clients. That I only half believed. Anyway, I already had a job and no desire to be steering filthy-rich characters around town, so I declined when she suggested I become her partner in this lucrative enterprise.

As I gradually left this nightlife behind, the world of mercenary sex faded from my view. To my great surprise, I have run into it again in my own political milieu—which I have called the *outre-gauche*, the "outer left." Among my comrades—anarchists or libertarian communists influenced by the Situationists—are two Polish girls who work happily as "mistresses," one in Paris, the other in Brussels. Meanwhile, in the United States, doctoral students of both sexes serve as escorts to well-heeled gents in order to pay off their student loans. Apart from simple financial considerations, this sort of thing certainly suggests a declaration of autonomy, of freedom. The same freedom defended by Grisélidis Réal, a leading light in the rebellion of sex workers in the 1970s, who held that prostitution freely exercised was "a revolutionary act" and "an Art, a Humanism, a Science." And this despite its ordinary and sordid aspects. Grisélidis was a writer, but she maintained that "streetwalking" was her second official profession. She fought her whole life long for the rights of prostitutes. In France today it is STRASS, the sex workers' union, that defends those freedoms.

There are also collectives, like that of the Chinese prostitutes of Belleville, the Roses d'Acier—Steel Roses—who fight against the police brutality to which they are prey. These women have had the courage not just to organize and fight for themselves, but also, on at least one occasion, to express their solidarity with migrants sleeping rough on the streets of Paris. In 2016, as we were marching with migrants from their camp in the Jardins d'Éole in northern Paris, twenty or so women of short stature, masked for anonymity and wearing miniskirts, fell in step with us and stayed with us for a good while. We decided that they could only be Steel Roses, and we were right: I happen to live near Belleville and habitually wave to prostitutes whom I often pass in the street, and now one or two of the pretty masked women marching alongside us greeted me in return.

But of course we all know what the condition of such women and of almost all prostitutes is really like. The criminalization of clients, as promoted by so-called abolitionists, can only reinforce the wretched lot of all who ply their trade in public. They are obliged to work in the shadows, putting themselves in harm's way by moving away from safer neighborhoods, and since johns then become more fearful, and rarer, and arrangements must be made more hastily, payments tend to be lowered and insistence on condom use abandoned. Prohibition and criminalization have never succeeded in eradicating prostitution. Sad to say, so long as money exists, heads, arms, and bodies will continue to be exploited, rented, and sold.

In May Do as You Will

In May 1968, I took part in the first demonstrations and the early occupation of the university. But inasmuch as I had already decided in April to leave Aix-en-Provence for good, I felt no particular pressure to continue occupying a department that had never been mine. My place was not in this bourgeois town with its students, even if I had friends among them: this was not the way I wanted to change the world. So I went back to Aubagne, to my parents, and there immediately joined an action committee that had just been formed by high schoolers, a few college students, and several workers, including a mailman, a plumber, and Pedro, the waiter at the café where we used to meet, as well as the owner's son, who tended bar. Amid the high school and student Trotskyists belonging to the JCR (Revolutionary Communist Youth) and the students and workers of the Maoist PCMLF (Marxist-Leninist Communist Party of France), Pedro—a son of Spanish émigrés—and I consti-tuted the anarchist contingent. Aubagne was a commune governed by the French Communist Party, and among the young Trotskyists in the action committee, several came from families who were party members, whom we dubbed Stalinists. Wherever the "Stals" and their trade union, the CGT (General Confederation of Labor), were powerful, their main concern was to prevent any contact between rebellious youth and "their" workers. Thus not a few local leaders found themselves challenged by their own children, which led to altercations as bitter as they were comical—even including the odd paternal slap across the face—as our action committee strove to join up with the striking *prolos* of one or another of the many factories in Aubagne and the Huveaune Valley. In any case, however, factory occupations—strikes and occupations being rife throughout the region—were tightly controlled by the Communists, and there was no chance at all of any damned "lefties" eroding union authority.

As for what we actually did in the action committee, I have no clear recollection. We had discussions, and we argued a great deal—hardly surprising in view of our disparate political allegiances. We tried to mobilize the town to little effect, and when we went to Marseille to protest, we never went as a group.

In that committee I made the acquaintance of Christian, a very young guy, barely fifteen, who was a leading figure locally in the JCR—later to morph into the Communist League and even later into the NPA (New Anticapitalist Party). A priori we had little in common, at least politically. But Christian was sharp, funny—and homosexual, which made him irresistible in my eyes. He fell for the radicalism of my views and the outlandishness of my outfits. I was certainly the only person who went to demonstrate in a yellow silk dress with mauve dots and a wide-brimmed violet hat. Christian soon became my coconspirator, and our friendship would endure for more than forty years, until the day his heart betrayed him prematurely in the middle of the street as he was on his way to La Ciotat's old port for an aperitif.

Christian was from a working-class family; his father was a stonemason. He had always known that he loved men,

Christian Pellegrini, circa 1992

and he made no secret of it. He had never set foot in a gay bar nor been confronted by homophobia. His unapologetic homosexuality contributed largely to his expulsion from the JCR a year after we met, although the official reason was "associating with anarcho-Maoists"—in other words, with me—which proved, if proof were needed, just how ignorant those Trotskyists were. It was true, however, that in the meantime I'd had him read the Situationists and his relationship with his comrades was seriously frayed.

In May, though Christian marched in Marseille with his organization, he and I often went in tandem to the almost-permanent agora set up near the Monument des Mobiles, a memorial to soldiers killed in the Franco-Prussian War of 1870, at the junction of La Canebière and Allée Léon-Gambetta. There you could find all sorts of people, everyone talking to one another, some getting up on their hind legs to improvise a speech or simply share what was on their mind—a startling and unprecedented scene. One heard the best, such as the young man haranguing the crowd: "For a year now psychiatrists have been keeping me stupefied, keeping me asleep. If we don't make this revolution now, I'll just be going back to sleep again." And also the worst, as for example an Indian from Pondicherry bemoaning France's abandonment of his homeland.

It was here—and certainly not at Lycée Thiers, named for the butcher of the Commune but now rechristened Lycée Commune de Paris, nor at the Saint-Charles faculty— here, well away from the unions and parties keeping such a tight rein on occupations and marches, that for us the true pulse of Marseille in revolt could be felt, here that we could fully relish the moment of elation that was May 1968. It must be said that Marseille, unlike other cities, did not experience barricades and clashes with the police: the "socialist" mayor Gaston Defferre cunningly contrived to avoid them by declaring his support for the movement. Demonstrations took the form of massive squadrooned marches, and woe betide anyone brave enough to challenge the CGT's marshals, mostly brawny dockworkers! Seeing Defferre appear on the balcony of City Hall flanked by two student-movement leaders let us take rather envious stock of the distance that separated us from the uprisings in Paris, Lyon, or Nantes.

Indeed, our "*joli mai*" ended without mayhem of any kind. The occupied university buildings, high schools, and factories eventually emptied out without police intervention. But I was not ready to give up the pleasure of the endless encounters and discussions to which the month of May had accustomed us. People everywhere had been talking to one another, confiding in one another, and expressing their wish to change their lives, to liberate themselves while drawing satisfaction from collective struggle. And this had been happening not just at the improvised assemblies in town and in workplaces, not just in occupied schools, but in exchanges on every street corner, in every shop, at every doorstep. At our naturist center, where strikers would come almost every day for lunch or just to pass a little time between two demonstrations or spells of occupation, debates—and fierce arguments—had continued incessantly, as in all families where parents and children are continually at loggerheads. We were not ready to abandon all of it just because the strikes and demonstrations had now ended.

For me the end of the movement was in fact the start of a new life, one ruled by the idea that the revolution was just round the corner—an idea I held dear for the next decade. After that it turned out the wait might be a little bit longer!

Meanwhile, in mid-June 1968, I took a job as a product demonstrator for the Berger company, a maker of pastis and fruit syrups. By a stroke of luck, my rounds took me to Avignon, where "cultural contestation" was in full swing. As soon as I got off work, I would plunge into hordes of young people intent on "making the revolution," many just down from Paris after having occupied the Théâtre de l'Odéon. What started things rolling was the banning of a play by Gérard Gelas, *La Paillasse aux seins nus* (The bare-breasted old whore), which Gelas's Chêne Noir company was supposed to put on, off-Festival, at the Chartreuse complex in Villeneuve. The organizers of the official program objected, and a protest meeting was called at the Place de l'Horloge, which was eventually broken up by a charge from the CRS riot police.

The Living Theatre, an "experimental libertarian troupe" from New York, had been invited to present their play *Paradise Now*—actually more a happening than a play—and their performers caused a scandal by stripping naked, canoodling, and mingling with the audience. We showed up en masse and tried to force our way into the Cloître des Célestins, where the piece was playing. Instead the actors came out and joined us, and it all ended with a raggedy demonstration in the streets of Avignon.

Among all the escapades of that hot summer, one of the most entertaining involved hiding about a hundred caged guinea fowl in a small townhouse near the Palace of the Popes and then releasing them onto the Palace stage, where Maurice Béjart's ballet company were performing *Messe pour le temps présent* (Mass for the present time). The occasion was a protest by the poultry farmers of the region. The sociologist Georges Lapassade, a vigorous supporter of this action who had once been lambasted by the Situationists ("*M. Lapassade est un con*"), was now redubbed "Professeur Lapintade"—Professor Guinea Fowl.

Although some of the dancers had been with us, Maurice Béjart himself took the thing very badly. This prompted us to come up with the slogan "Vilar—Béjart—Salazar," which was misguided to say the least. But we feared nothing, not even making fools of ourselves—and we had to be really foolish to liken Jean Vilar and Maurice

Béjart to the repulsive Portuguese dictator. But I should probably say no more, because after a night locked up by the cops I'm afraid I assaulted poor Vilar on the pretext that he had somehow been involved in the arrests.

Before I continued my circuit for Berger, there was time for me to be pursued by a bunch of goons out to terrorize us. They had already attacked the Living Theatre people, injuring some of them, and done violence to friends of ours, including a young guy from Marseille whom they beat up, shaving his head with a knife and leaving him unconscious on the banks of the Rhône. I was on my way back to the little hotel where my employers had put me up when a gang of these goons started chasing me. I locked myself in a toilet just inside the hotel entrance, and they were trying to break the door down when suddenly I heard them take off running. It turned out I owed my skin to the fact that they thought they had roused the hotel's owner; in reality it was a pair of male guests who had been disturbed by the noise and started down the stairs—one of Béjart's dancers and a journalist from (I think) *Le Nouvel Observateur*.

The next summer, the summer of the Gainsbourg and Birkin hit "69 année érotique," I went back to Avignon and ended up sleeping under the stars with a very motley crew on a little island in the middle of the Rhône. Aside from the comrades who had come from Aix with me and a few hippies from Denmark, Holland or various parts of France, there were some from Nantes and Bordeaux who had been involved in the two most far-reaching episodes of student radicalism outside of Paris: in both their cities, back in 1967, young people influenced by the ideas of the Situationist International had succeeded in getting themselves elected to the leadership of UNEF (National

Student Union of France) and seizing control of its various subdivisions; in this they were following the example set the year before by the Strasbourg students who had used UNEF funds to publish the pamphlet *De la misère en milieu étudiant*, which, as noted earlier, had such a decisive influence on me. In Bordeaux the rebels called themselves "Vandalists" and used this moniker to sign their notorious broadside *Crève Salope!* (Die, scum!), in which they anathematized all authority figures, parents, teachers, doctors, and *tutti quanti*. Although the exploits of the Strasbourg students of 1966 had been brought to an end fairly soon by means of legal reprisals, those young revolutionaries bore not a little responsibility for the radical turn taken later in Nantes and Bordeaux. Likewise in Lyon, where the local chapter of the March 22 Movement, considerably more militant than its model in Nanterre, took the lead.*

Long story short, it was with enthusiasm that I joined up with the Nantes and Bordeaux folks on that island in 1969, far away this year from the cultural agitation of the Avignon Festival. For us the issue now was the emancipation of everyone: time to start "changing life" *hic et nunc*. And first and foremost changing our own lives—by way, in our eyes, of setting an example. This led us to organize various public demonstrations—notably against the fascists, whose violent attacks seemed not to have ceased since the previous year—and to fuel outrage at every opportunity. We would confront passersby and hurl invectives at priests, bourgeois, cops, and soldiers. As we were getting stoned a lot, smoking hash, taking speed,

---

* I have collected many memories of the period from *soixante-huitards* active in the French provinces in my *Voyage en outre-gauche: Paroles de francs-tireurs des années 68* (Voyage through the outer left: Sharpshooters of '68 speak) (Paris: Libertalia, 2018).

and passing round an ether-soaked blanket to sniff, we tended to carry our provocations very far, including sexual ones, which the gay men hardly shrank from. For my part I made love with my new boyfriend from Bordeaux in broad daylight on Place de l'Horloge, covered by nothing but a pareo that concealed barely any of our frolics. On that little island we changed the world and balled a lot, creating a kind of enchanted parenthesis that was brutally closed the day one of our number drowned before our eyes in the Rhône.

Right after that I left for Paris, where I had already spent several months the previous fall. I soon made the Place de la Contrescarpe my base of operations. This hilltop in the Latin Quarter, familiarly known as "La Mouffe" after Rue Mouffetard, which crosses the Contrescarpe, was the evening gathering place for all of Paris's young revolutionaries, organized or not, along with myriad birds of passage. A whiff of May '68 was still in the air, and an atmosphere of rebellion and nonstop festivity reigned. One could always find a way to eat, a place to sleep at someone or other's, and above all allies and coconspirators for actions invariably conceived as "radical and coherent." We took part in demonstrations, with or without rioting and pillage, and dreamt up collective and communal schemes, many of which would die the death much later on in the Cévennes. There was even an ephemeral and entertaining Mouffe Liberation Front, whose most famous exploit was the theft of several baskets of oysters on display outside a restaurant and their subsequent sampling in the street.

Amid this maelstrom, in a little group of dissident anarchists with whom I had been hanging out for a while, I found Agathe, from the South of France like me, and like me homeless and rootless in Paris. Agathe was from a poor and joyless family, and she had had to leave school very early. So she was by no means an "intellectual," but her view of the world was more intelligent and clear-sighted than any I had yet encountered then. Which is certainly why, after we combined our wanderings, I formed an irreversible attachment to her. We quickly became the best of friends, as we still are to this day.

(Poly)sexual Explosion

In Marseille, to which I returned for a time, as in all big university towns, the municipality had made a building available to the student union. In this case, the union was AGEM (General Association of Marseille Students), headed at the time by the bizarre Trotsko-Luxemburgist "Groupe 66." The building, in the Allées Meilhan at the very top of La Canebière, contained offices, meeting rooms, copying machines, a bar on the ground floor, and a nightclub in the basement. The police could enter only by permission of the rector. The AGEM bar became a favorite haunt for Christian and me. Soon I ran into two lesbian friends there, Lucille from high school days and Pascale from my childhood.

Since my departure for Paris, young opponents of both the Stalinists of the Communist Party and the various Leninist groups had begun to organize, and I immediately found a place in their ranks. Half-jokingly, we called this informal alliance of ours the "hyper-left"—a label that inspired me fifty years later to coin the term *outre-gauche* (or "outer left") to designate the heterogeneous tendency that stretches from anarchists unaffiliated with the Fédération Anarchiste, via the Situationists, to left communists of various stripes.

Raising high the banner of the critique of everyday life after our own fashion, and indeed often in ways far removed from the original conception, a good many of us gave ourselves over to urban *dérives*, to the consumption of all sorts of drugs, and to liberated sex. All of which was supposed to contribute, along with more straightforward political theory and practice, to the imminent destruction of the old world.

At a time when syphilis was no longer a serious threat and AIDS still unheard of, we discovered that theoretical harmony and sensual harmony were inseparable and that, as a slogan of May '68 had it, "the more you make the revolution, the more you make love." And vice versa.

Like the oppression of women, the repression of homosexuality got short shrift in the struggles of May. True, there was an ephemeral Revolutionary Pederastic Action Committee at the Sorbonne, but that was about it. There wasn't much by way of feminism either. Granted, this was not a time of separate struggles, and even less of identitarian ones. But the aftermath of May witnessed, within the general emancipatory movement, a blooming of the desire for a free amorous and sexual life in the immediate moment and without waiting for the revolution. In Marseille, as no doubt elsewhere, we wanted to live and love each other "without dead time and without constraint," as Vaneigem puts it—without the fetters of coupledom, without succumbing to exclusiveness. All sorts of relationships sprang up in a fluid way and we soon began, quite spontaneously, to engage in group sex. In what we called "the heap," everything was permitted: it was sensual, tender, and also very joyful. A heap was never obligatory, nor was it organized, save perhaps in the last few moments, when we had to find a bed or room large enough to accommodate our collective lovemaking. At times several of us might get into bed together just to cuddle up and even sleep there with nothing sexual going on. This all came about as a natural extension of our shared life. It was in one such heap that I met Vivian, an intermittent lover and a lifelong friend. When he joined us, I barely knew him. He arrived with a boy whose lover he was; I had come with Christian and some other boys and girls. We all fooled around a lot. Christian convinced a little fair-haired guy, who was a newbie in the group, that I was his, Christian's, older sister, which got the guy extraordinarily excited. We combined and recombined a great deal one night, and by dawn there were only four of us left in the bed, Christian with the blond boy, and I with Vivian. Almost half a century later, when Vivian's children asked us how we first met, we didn't dare tell them.

In the late 1970s, Vivian opened a bar with a bunch of friends on Rue Sainte in Marseille. The place was a great success, and its clientele went far beyond our little "hyper-left" circle. It was known as "Le VV," although there was no sign. Customers took the name to mean approximately "look-look," because in Marseille dialect *vé*, derived from the Provençal *vèïre*, means "see." Only the initiated knew that VV really stood for *la voile et la vapeur*, "sail and steam," or, as Americans would say, AC/DC. What better way to salute bisexuality, especially in the context of Marseille bistrology?

It was a good thing that we knew how to share a bed in a higgledy-piggledy way, because in July 1970 Yves (my Parisian partner), Christian, Harpo and Jojo (two other friends from Marseille), Lucille, and I all arrived in Pyla, a small seaside resort with posh villas on Arcachon Bay, at a large house all of whose bedrooms were already taken. No one invited us to share a room or a bed, even though we had with us Lucille's baby daughter, Juliette, who was only ten months old. So we purloined a few mattresses and set up a fine communal sleeping area in the middle of the living room—a space that the others instantly nicknamed "the Raft of the *Medusa*." Then we ensconced "our" baby in a large armoire alongside us after emptying it and making it comfortable for her. The others at the house for the meeting must have scratched their heads at the sight of this crew made up of two guys claiming to be gay, another supposedly bisexual, a lesbian mother with her baby, and a straight couple refusing to be a couple, all sleeping together on their "raft."

The villa had been rented by IDHEC (Institute for Advanced Cinematographic Studies) as a location for Alain Montesse, known as Matou, to shoot his thesis film.

There were a good thirty of us, even more at times, young men and women all more or less influenced by left communism and by the Situationists and hailing from every corner of France, Italy and Belgium, as well as an Algerian, a Czech Jew, an Englishman who was in charge of the production and hence the budget, a Swiss filmmaker, and an American deserter joined for a few days by two or three others who refused like him to fight in Vietnam.

Things were pretty chaotic at first. Apart from getting settled, we had to make sure not to run out of food, and more importantly out of drink. We fought regularly with the Vandalists from Bordeaux over our wine stocks and over the comparative revolutionary radicalism of our positions. We burst into rooms where "little couples"—a pejorative label if ever there was one—had closeted themselves in search of intimacy and "seclusion." "But seclusion from what?" (or words to that effect) we cried to anyone within earshot. Our disputes soon turned raucous, especially when we suddenly noticed a microphone being lowered towards us from upstairs. Of course there was recording and film equipment all over the place—natural enough, surely, considering that playacting both cinematic and figurative was the order of the day. Our discussions became ever more fraught as we got to wondering why we had all been brought together. We decided to call a meeting to clear things up. Matou and the English guy did not attend—they must have been too busy snooping on us with their mics and cameras. It turned out that each of our little groups had been given a different reason for their presence: Matou had told some that the idea was to build a network designed to launch linked and simultaneous actions in each of the places we came from; others had been informed that the aim was to work together on the development of a new theory of revolution; yet a third group understood that we were to experiment with a new lifestyle; and as for us, we learnt that we would be meeting interesting people, drinking, eating, and having fun, all courtesy of IDHEC.

In the end it was a bit of all of the above, but at the same time we began talking in a genuinely serious way, we built relationships, many of which were to endure, and we went and disturbed municipal festivities in Arcachon, cutting off the power and creating all kinds of supposedly subversive situations. To top things off, there was a great geographico-amorous reshuffling: one Bordeaux girl went off to Paris with a Savoyard, another followed an Italian back to Naples, and a Parisian went to live in Belgium with the hitherto partner of the Neapolitan. I had a furtive affair with a Vandalist, Christian had a chance to perfect his English, Yves came to blows with some people from Le Havre, and Jojo contemplated marrying Lucille so that baby Juliette, "father unknown," would acquire a dad in the eyes of the State. Much to our regret, this did not come about. We would have so loved to be avant-garde enough to have a family among us with a lesbian mother and a queer father.

All told, our Pyla sojourn gave rise to a number of durable friendships, romances, and political bonds, thus far surpassing Matou's original plan, which, as I learnt not long ago, was that the "wild general assembly" he had created would appropriate the moviemaking tools and document the radicalism of the times. As for his thesis film, the pretext for our gathering, I never saw anything but rushes, although Matou did go on to make some experimental films, including *Les Situs heureux* (Happy Situationists), screened continuously at the Paris gallery La Maison Rouge during a catchall exhibition in 2017 called *L'esprit français, contre-cultures (1968–1989)*, which claimed to commemorate the fiftieth anniversary of May '68.

Once back in Paris, Yves, Christian, Jojo and I decided to rent an apartment and make a group life there. At a moment when we thought that those of our friends who had chosen to go to the Cévennes to live communally and make goat cheese were deserters, what we aspired to be was a group devoted to life, action, and theory—and above all not a "community," for in our eyes a community could only mean a "community of impoverishment."

We set up home in a three-room flat in Rue Fagon, near Place d'Italie, where we were soon joined by Elsa and Annabelle, two girls from the Censier "base group," a post-May action committee, one of whose organizers was Guy Hocquenghem, later a prominent figure in the gay movement. Then came another Christian, known as "Black Christian" because he was very dark and very anarchist, and Marc, from Nantes, whom I knew from our island camp in Avignon. Alban arrived from Tunisia with

Hassan, his young lover, while others visited briefly from time to time, and yet others, like the two buddies known as "Mandrin" and "Jacob," nicknamed respectively for the eighteenth-century smuggler Louis Mandrin and the anarchist burglar Marius (Alexandre) Jacob, came by almost every day. The apartment soon became a meeting place and a place of welcome. A friend from Aix sent us a tall, charismatic Black guy from Amsterdam who needed cheering up; he had fled South Africa after challenging apartheid by founding a racially mixed anarchist group. A stone's throw away was another tribe, and in a maid's room on the top floor of our building lived a young fishmonger who had plenty of good-looking pals. Alain Pacadis, future punk chronicler of the Paris underground scene and author of the "Clubbing" column in *Libération*, had been a member of the Censier base group with Elsa and Annabelle, which explains why he often came by Rue Fagon to parade his faded dandified clothes and his equally faded persona. And with the key always being in the apartment door, intense young people of both sexes would show up at all hours.

All these fine-feathered folks had to be fed, but as a matter of fact we ate rather well because we preferred to steal quality food. We drank a good deal, smoked joints and occasionally dropped acid. To cover the rent and our other overheads, we were obliged to work—as little as possible, of course. Yves and I did market surveys, and Elsa and Annabelle supervised little kids at a school canteen, while the two Christians worked a bit as mail sorters. As for Jojo, who had attended a school of mines in an earlier life, he scored an extraordinary sinecure at the CNRS (National Center for Scientific Research): as the sole scientist in a literature department, he was tasked, in those almost prehistoric days of the computer revolution, with digitizing and archiving successive transcriptions of Cicero's writings so that alterations in them could be tracked. What this meant in practice was that he was barely ever seen at the research lab but that his pay raised our standard of living considerably. Hassan, who had been supported financially by Alban in Tunisia, startled us by getting a job in a pizzeria, which enabled him to return the favor. Mandrin and Jacob, true to their nicknames, were thieves: they ripped books off from stores and sold them for the most part to students at the left-leaning Vincennes university center, a place where none of us would ever have set foot without a good reason, so thoroughly did we hate professors and students alike, especially the Maoists and Trotskyists who proliferated there.

Of our three rooms we set aside two as common sleeping quarters and reserved the third for meals, discussion, and flights of fancy. Its walls were covered with kraft paper on which everyone was invited to express themselves by writing or drawing. In the bedrooms we could merely sleep together or engage in erotic activity with whomever we pleased, two or more at a time. Nothing was mandated, and each followed their inclinations. We championed complete romantic and erotic freedom and wanted to believe we could accept and practice anything. We no longer wished to be homo- or hetero- or even bisexual: our project was to be pansexual, although for us this did not include such things as pedophilia or zoophilia—possibilities that in fact never entered our heads. None of us had formed the concept of "polysexuality," although it would certainly have fitted the bill.

This was the background against which Christian one day expressed his frustration at not being able to make love with a woman. Men, of course, were what attracted

him, but all the same this shortcoming was unacceptable
to him. During long discussions of our desires and our
sexuality, Christian told us how, when he was about five,
he had been caught by a neighbor engaging in sexual play
with the man's little daughter. He still remembered the
father threatening to hang both of them by their ears from
a clothesline and, in particular, to cut off his dick. As if to
fulfill some psychoanalyst's dream of at last unearthing a
primal trauma, Christian succeeded just a few days after
this confession in making love with Annabelle. He didn't
become any straighter as a result, but inasmuch as he was
able thereafter, two or three times, to have sexual relations
with women, he was reassured that his love for men was
not the outcome of some kind of inhibition. By contrast,
Marc delightedly discovered his bisexuality, Yves hewed
fast to his straightness, and I myself made new discoveries
about women. We suffered outbreaks of pubic lice and
then scabies, both of which I miraculously escaped, but I
could not prevent my long hair from playing host to the
nits that Elsa and Annabelle were forever bringing home
from their school canteen.

A casual visitor to our abode might have been forgiven
for concluding that all we ever did was gab, stuff ourselves,
and fuck. In point of fact, however, we were always more
or less on high alert. Out in the street we went on long
dérives after the fashion of the Situationists, and we
strove to provoke and mix it up at every opportunity.
We believed that living as a group entailed group action,
and you have to remember that this was a time of great
turbulence when it came to ideas, debate, and action. We
demonstrated, supported the strikers at the mail-sorting
center where the two Christians had worked, and could
be found wherever there was trouble. We aspired to fight

on all fronts, and naturally we were deeply involved in the struggles against the oppression of women, for the right to abortion, and against sexual repression, especially with regard to homosexuality.

One day a girl we were friendly with took us to a meeting of the MLF (Women's Liberation Movement) in an auditorium in the fifteenth arrondissement—this was probably before their assemblies at the École des Beaux-Arts, or else at the same time, I just can't remember. Since men were not allowed, Elsa, Annabelle and I left the guys at a café across the street. Soon after we joined the meeting, we tried to explain that we lived in a group with men both straight and gay, that we could not imagine any struggle without them, and that for us the emancipation of women could not come about in isolation from the emancipation of everyone, all sexual tendencies included. We were brusquely silenced and told in no uncertain terms that the single-sex nature of the assembly was not to be contested.

As the meeting went on, we wondered more and more what we were doing there. First of all, it was obvious right away that amid all these young women, dressed casually, but chic, with hippie or flapper touches, we seemed like pathetic slobs in flea-market clothes that were far from fashionable and certainly not ironed. Then we heard a stuck-up creature in a tweed jacket, a white shirt, and impeccable flannel pants announce that she was "a lesbian by political choice." As with one voice, we cried, "Oh yeah? Not for the pleasure of it, you poor fool?"—or something to that effect. We had said our piece, and it was as plain as day that this event, led by bourgeois ideologues, was not for us. When we rejoined "our" guys in the café opposite, we realized it was full of other men obediently waiting for their women to come out.

Meanwhile Génia, my mom, cut herself off forever from the celebration of Mother's Day by handing out the official MLF paper *Le Torchon Brûle* (The flaming dishrag),* in whose pages this holiday, once promoted by Marshal Pétain, was quite rightly denounced. The result was a new balance in the household, because my father had always rejected Father's Day—in his view a pure invention of shopkeepers. He had likewise refused to let me believe in Santa Claus: why should he put in overtime just to buy me presents for which I would thank "an old geezer who doesn't even exist"?

There were ever more denizens in our three-room-with-kitchen in Rue Fagon. It was getting really tight, and some of us began to talk about finding another place. That was when a guy who had been close to the Vandalists brought in three youngsters from well-to-do families. One of them, who stood to inherit a fortune, had the bright idea of presenting the group with a gold ingot, actually a birthday present from his grandmother. This sparked a wild outbreak of rapacity: Mandrin and Jacob were frantic with excitement, our whole little world was in an uproar— in short, the atmosphere turned really putrid. The heir was not yet twenty-one and could not sell the ingot himself, so Alban made the sale and paid off his overdraft with part of the proceeds, after which Hassan and he left the sinking ship. Returning from a trip, Yves and I discovered the disaster and played the new broom by sweeping out everyone who to whatever degree had fallen to worshipping the golden calf—or rather the golden ingot. We ended

---

* Originally this expression meant that torches were lit, so trouble was brewing. The more modern sense of *torchon* as a dishrag has added a domestic resonance to the phrase. —Trans.

up with our original hard core and a few newcomers. It was time for a change. We decided to break up but maintain close relations. Yves, Marc, and I attempted a ménage à trois—not very successfully, it must be said, for Yves remained resolutely straight. We took an apartment on Rue Charlemagne in the Marais, which was not yet either a posh neighborhood or the epicenter of the Parisian gay world. It was an apartment where we knew we could contest the rent, and hence postpone its payment, on the grounds that the toilet opened illegally into the kitchen—which incidentally gave rise to a great debate over whether or not to leave its door open when we used it.

There, too, the key was always in the door as an invitation to whatever adventures still awaited us.

Workers of the World, Group Grope!

It was natural enough that in April 1971 we joined the FHAR (Homosexual Revolutionary Action Front), which had just been founded and had already made a reputation for itself by interrupting a radio program, broadcast directly from the Salle Pleyel, entitled "Homosexuality: A Grievous Problem." The name this little group chose for itself made it clear from the start that it was not a homosexual rights movement but a revolutionary front organized by homosexuals. Which was just fine with Jojo, Christian and the others, for they did not want to be defined by their sexual orientation but treated as "revolutionaries" who, like women revolutionaries, simply had to contend with an extra layer of repression. For us it was out of the question to support any *exclusive* struggle at all.

The FHAR had been started by lesbians, so there were a good many women involved at the time; all sexual orientations were represented, and polysexuality was the watchword. This could not have suited us better, not least because, though May '68 was only a couple of years in the past, not so many people shared our views.

Once we had settled into Rue Charlemagne—and "settled" is saying a lot, because we had barely more than mattresses on the floor, a table, a few stools, a rack for our clothes, and a couple of multipurpose crates—we helped set up an FHAR committee in the Marais district, took part in actions at gay hangouts, where we sought to persuade the queers and dykes to come out of their ghetto and join us, and took part in a variety of demonstrations. A high point was the organization's attack on the gay bashers of Buttes-Chaumont: Françoise d'Eaubonne, writer and cofounder of the FHAR, led the pack as, spurred on by the shrill cries of the queens, they fell upon those thugs and to their amazement beat the shit out of them in a respectably macho way.

The FHAR's pride and joy was our general assemblies at the École des Beaux-Arts, which unfolded in remarkable disarray. The floor belonged to whoever shouted the loudest, had the most resounding arguments, or jumped up on the table bare naked to make themselves heard. This meant that speech was truly spontaneous and its possibilities very broad. There was no leader, which was what we wanted. When some would-be leaders tried to take over, we unfurled a good kilometer's worth of toilet paper (pink, of course) over the gathering to let our disapproval be known.

Amid all this, I fell in love with a delightful young woman named Micheline. Ready to do anything to please her, I let her drag me to a meeting of the Gouines Rouges (Red Dykes). Right away I felt uncomfortable and somewhat confused in the face of a fervent audience being hectored with overbearing authority by a few tough dykes. Suddenly the door opened and through it barged one of the draggiest of the FHAR's queens. He was looking for his coat, left behind in the room after an earlier event. This very effeminate young guy was greeted by a storm of jeers: it was absolutely unacceptable that a *man* should enter, if only for a moment. This enraged me, and I shouted with all my might that the comrade was anything but an enemy and that plenty of the females there were far more "manly" than him. I fetched the said coat, grabbed the hand of my girlfriend, who was just as outraged as I was, and announced that we were taking our FHAR comrade for the drink he certainly needed by now. Lo and behold, several women attendees fell in with us as we left. End of conversation with those "red" lesbians.

Meanwhile things were going south at the FHAR too. There were fewer and fewer women, and our assemblies were tending to turn into beauty contests and pickup venues for orgies upstairs. And artists and writers would attend just to drum up business for their galleries and theaters, and if we later interrupted their events in protest, they would call us police provocateurs. When they rebuked us for heckling in the theater or scrawling FAGS ARE VANDALS on paintings, we retorted that as merchandisers of homosexuality they had only themselves to blame and that they had one hell of a nerve inviting us to their trendy events. It is true, of course, that this was just a foretaste of what the radiant future had in store for us in the way of targeted marketing.

Some people—like Guy Hocquenghem, though he changed his mind later—promoted the notion that homosexuality was revolutionary per se because it challenged the basis of our society, namely the family and its reproduction. The homosexual thus became a revolutionary subject, if not *the* revolutionary subject, whereby the capitalist world would be destroyed. But how could bisexuality *not* be co-optable? "What?" was our retort. "Are you saying there was no such thing as a gay Nazi?" Meanwhile, if being homosexual was "a political choice"—a claim I had heard among the Gouines Rouges—we were miles away indeed from the free and multifarious sexuality we were fighting for.

I admit that at the time I paid no attention to the theories of "materialist feminism" being developed by Christine Delphy and Monique Wittig, both cofounders of the Gouines Rouges. Defining women as a "group" and a "class," the argument was, in Wittig's words, that the category of women "has no meaning outside heterosexual systems of thought and economics. Lesbians are not women." The question here was thus not sexual orientation properly speaking but rather a particularized approach to struggle—an approach that I have never espoused myself, on account of its sectional and hermetic nature.

The FHAR assemblies were also plagued by the machinations of little Hitlers grandfathered in from leftist groups and marked by their bureaucratic training. We soon became aware that they were making decisions in advance and viewed debate at our general assembly as nothing but a rubber stamp. The upshot was that actions undertaken by the FHAR became more and more manipulated and more and more policed. For instance, when the organization took part in a rally organized by the MLF against Mother's Day on the Pelouse de Reuilly in the Bois de Vincennes, we found ourselves so constrained by these bureaucratic elements that no spontaneous action was possible. We also found out that they were maintaining a secret filing system and had arrogated to themselves the right to sort and respond to the organization's mail. They took control of our relations with the paper *Tout!*, which then published a selection of our letters. *Tout!* was a periodical close to the "Mao-Spontex" tendency and had devoted an issue to the FHAR, implying that we demanded "the right to homosexuality and to all homosexualities" as well as "the right of minors to the free expression and fulfilment of their [sexual] desires." This earned Jean-Paul

Sartre, then the formal editor of the paper, an indictment for "offending public decency."

For us this was the last straw, and eight of us, two women and six men, signed a statement with our full names (unlike the customary "a member of the FHAR" or other anonymous or pseudonymous attributions). Our title was "Et voilà pourquoi votre fille est muette" (And that's why your daughter is dumb).* After declaring that "the liberation of homosexuals will not be the work of homosexuals alone," we announced our resignation from the FHAR, which had "become a ghetto and a creator of ghettos," and invited "those who desire the FHAR's self-transcendence" to meet with us and "require that the overall problem of relationships be put on the table and a resolution sought that must absolutely be revolutionary in nature." The language is dated, and reading it now brings a nostalgic smile to my lips. That said, considering what later became of some of the members of the FHAR, I can only congratulate us in retrospect for quitting. This was really brought home to me in 1981, when a bash organized by the magazine *Gai Pied* at Le Palace nightclub turned into a booster for François Mitterand's campaign for the presidency of the republic. The event was meant mostly as a thank-you for Mitterand's promise to repeal the despicable antihomosexual laws of Pétain and de Gaulle. That promise was kept, but it was soon plain that, among the many former Maoists and Trotskyists who in Guy Hocquenghem's words slid "from Mao jackets to the Rotary Club," there were a good many ex-FHARists

---

* A line from Molière's farce *Le Médecin malgré lui* (The doctor in spite of himself) that has become a French catchphrase. The remark concludes a charlatan's stream of pseudo-medical gobbledygook. —Trans.

eager to accept the posts, sinecures, and honors on offer from the administration of a politician who not only had a part in the Vichy government but oversaw the murderous repression of Algerian freedom fighters. So much for the "Tonton mania" cult of Mitterrand as an avuncular figure. And so much for "revolutionary action"!

After we broke with the FHAR, our apartment in Rue Charlemagne saw intense activity and traffic in and out on the part of many comrades of both sexes, some of whom continued to attend the FHAR's general assemblies. Oddly, the increasingly unfettered sex and the consumption of hallucinogenic drugs seemed merely to bolster our energy and combativeness. Those were splendid times, our high spirits knew no bounds, and we were in harmony.

Within the FHAR we had found our soul sisters in the shape of the Gazolines, an informal group of girls and queens; several of the latter transitioned later. What we had in common with the Gazolines was the rejection of all little Hitlers and a taste for general subversion. One of their number, and not the least, who would work later as a journalist under the name of Hélène Hazera, was a regular visitor to Rue Charlemagne. Much influenced by the Situationists, she was a little bit younger than me, intelligent, cultured, very radical and very pretty. In a recent interview she confessed that for her the Gazolines were motivated mainly by "the desire to piss people off"—a rather blunt way of evoking the group's opposition to those "leftists" who sought to control the movement and make it seem serious and respectable.

Hélène and I were great friends, and we still are. I remember how she used to begin phone calls to me by playing Marlene Dietrich singing "Lili Marleen" or "Ich bin die fesche Lola" so I would know who was on the line.

Demonstrating with the Gazolines was a blast, not least on account of their improbable slogans: "Makeup First and Foremost," "Leftists, Untighten Your Asses," "Up the Ass—How Good It Is!" or the memorable "Workers of the World, Group Grope!" invented by Hélène. They all delighted me.

With my new partner, Donatien, I accompanied the Gazolines to the burial of Pierre Overney, a Maoist militant murdered by a security guard while passing out leaflets at the nationalized Renault automobile plant. Aware that the Maoists were "minting money off their martyr," ginning up support by means of this highly publicized ceremony, the Gazolines pretended to be weepers as the cortège headed for the Père-Lachaise Cemetery. I was so impressed that I came to believe in memory that they had actually dressed up in widow's mourning clothes—until Hélène dismissed this as pure fantasy. I cannot have been the only person to fantasize about it, however, because a "lightly veiled widow" appears in Frédéric Martel's book *Le Rose et le noir* (The pink and the black). So widespread was disapproval of the Gazolines' behavior that it even called down the anathema of the eminent Daniel Guérin, writer, historian, theoretician of libertarian Marxism, and venerable homosexual activist born in 1904, who deemed it "disgusting to bare one's backside at a funeral."

Little by little a passionate love affair with Donatien drew me away from Rue Charlemagne and the remnants of the FHAR, though not from my friends and our fight against sexual codes and roles. The effervescence was on the wane, but we were still convinced that revolution was in the offing. There were many fewer strikes and demonstrations, to be sure, but everything was continuing in a low-key way, or so we believed, between two great surges.

Since there was relatively little by way of "militant" action, we began, without ever making any formal decision, to spend more time reading, theorizing, and putting out flyers, periodicals and pamphlets. We also traveled, and we met new comrades almost everywhere. In 1974 many of us were in Portugal for the so-called Carnation Revolution, while I was with Donatien and a few close friends in an Italy then in a high state of political agitation. In Spain still others were conducting clandestine operations against the Franco regime. The Hippie Trail to Afghanistan and Kathmandu was decidedly not on our itinerary.

Through my favorite Vandalist, Arthur, we got to know the left-communist publisher René Lefeuvre, founder of Éditions Spartacus. Lefeuvre published texts that confirmed our critique of the USSR and its state capitalism, broadened our knowledge of revolutionary movements from the Paris Commune to the Spanish Civil War via the Kronstadt Rebellion and the German Revolution, nourished our interest in German-Dutch oppositional communism, and in many ways informed our theoretical vision of revolution, even if we were frequently at odds with him.

René's small apartment in Rue Sainte-Croix-de-la-Bretonnerie, where two or three handsome young men were always in residence, was chockablock with books and prints. Any visit put you in danger of having to schlep books around, fold and gather sheets, wrap packages, do secretarial work, or perform a host of other tasks for which René always needed more hands on deck. And if you were able, you would also be called upon to write, translate, and offer ideas for new publications. All of which fell to us on occasion. Our recompense would be a delicious dinner—invariably roast pork and rice.

René Lefeuvre, 1979

René was homosexual, and he claimed never to
have fallen in love with any woman aside from Rosa
Luxemburg—and that was of course an imaginary love.
No wonder, then, that there was a good vibe between
us from the start and that his homosexuality tended to
underpin our long conversations. René confided in me
that he had long hidden, even stifled, his love for men. It
would have been perilous for him to come out as a young
stonemason in Brittany in the 1920s, but it was no easier
to do so even after he became a Parisian, a proofreader
and a political militant. One can only conclude that the
left-Marxist milieu, even in its ultra versions, remained

just as puritanical and norm-ridden in this regard as the French Communist Party. One thinks of Engels's denunci-ation of "the Greeks' repugnant practice of pederasty" or, to a lesser degree perhaps, of Wilhelm Reich's dismissal of homosexuality as a neurosis—in sharp contrast to Freud's view that it was merely "a variant of the sexual function."

Both Communists and many Marxist-Leninists considered homosexuals a danger to the party or organiza-tion on the grounds that they were susceptible to blackmail and hence security risks. Beneath this seemingly rational argument, however, there surely lay an embrace of "revolu-tionary virtue" dating back to the day when homosexuality was dubbed a "bourgeois vice."

More generally speaking, all serious militants were supposed to forgo pleasure, especially pleasure deemed illegal or simply discountenanced by their organization. In the early 1970s, a friend of ours, a worker, sought to join the "Bordigists"—a left-communist tendency distin-guished by its insistence on the need for a party and so named because it adhered to the theories of Amadeo Bordiga, a cofounder of the Italian Communist Party later expelled for his opposition to Stalin. At his very first meeting, our friend was informed that militants must not drink or smoke so as not to incapacitate themselves and jeopardize their commitment. No mention was made of sexual relations, but it was quite clear that any attempt on his part to find girlfriends within the group would be unacceptable. I can't imagine what would have transpired had he sought out a *male* lover among those Bordigists!

The JCR, just after its mutation into the Communist League, carried out a widespread purge in Marseille. My friend Christian, who had never concealed his homosex-uality, was given the boot along with a young Arab who smoked dope and a girl whose favorite pastime was to lay every leader who passed through. As so well summed up by the Organization of Young Revolutionary Workers (OJTR) in their collective pamphlet *Militantism, Highest Stage of Alienation* (1972), the militant "is separated from his own desires."

It was Daniel Guérin who liberated René Lefeuvre and helped him become fully himself. Subsequently René profited as much as he could from this development and went regularly to the Arcadie club, whose weekly balls he particularly enjoyed. René was never a member of the FHAR, but he joined Arcadie, a homosexual association founded in the 1950s that cultivated discretion and respectability. This I found outrageous, and one day I rebuked René about it more vehemently than was my wont: "How can you," I asked him, "as a homosexual and a revolutionary, choose to belong to a law-abiding bourgeois institution concerned above all with its good reputation?" René replied tearfully: "You don't understand what this means to me. It was at Arcadie that I was able for the first time in my life to dance with a man." In my impetuousness I had been utterly insensitive. Luckily René did not hold it against me. He was a man of an earlier day and, unlike Daniel Guérin, could never absorb the idea that a transgressive sexuality could also be a political weapon.

Damned Viruses

By the early 1980s, hope for revolution was distinctly on the ebb. This was the end of the "May '68" years in France, the "years of lead" in Italy, and the "transition to democracy" in Spain and Portugal. I resigned myself to taking a full-time job at a market research firm.

In 1984, AIDS, the "homosexual plague," was visited upon my entourage. The firm where I had recently started working employed a couple of young guys as freelancers. Since I had too much work, I proposed to Paul, one of them, that he work with me full time. He accepted right away, but a fortnight later he announced that there was no point in it because he had AIDS and it made no sense for him to embark on a "career" now that his death was imminent. Let me hasten to soften this by saying right away that Paul is still among us today thanks to the ever more effective treatments that he followed faithfully, and he continued freelancing until his retirement. On the other hand, his partner was carried off after just a year.

People were only just beginning to talk about AIDS in the early 1980s. Medical knowledge was still in its infancy, and public knowledge virtually nonexistent. The most fantastical theories and rumors about the disease's transmission proliferated wildly. You heard claims that you could catch AIDS from a subway or movie-theater seat, or from a toilet, or from a badly washed glass. So

I was concerned about the reaction at the office. It was not unusual, even in that predominantly female and supposedly enlightened professional environment, for HIV-positive employees to be discriminated against and even let go. This was especially easy with freelancers, for it was just a matter of not calling on them. To my great relief, however, solidarity at our company was total. It turned out that the brother-in-law of one of our female colleagues had died from AIDS and the parents had taken in and cared for the man's partner, whom his own family had rejected. This was sad, of course, but scarcely out of the ordinary: so many young men, infected or simply suspect on account of their homosexuality, were renounced by their parents, their brothers and sisters, even their friends, for fear of contagion, shame, or some simply irrational impulse. One has to remember that early in the epidemic there was no known treatment, no clear distinction was drawn between seropositivity and active AIDS, and a swift and painful death was forecast for anyone testing positive. Nevertheless, everyone—from our very young secretary newly arrived from central France, sweet but fairly naive and conventional, to our boss, a very rigid Dane—behaved in a perfectly natural way, and the notion of a risk of contamination, whether by direct contact or by way of the dishes, for instance, was never to my knowledge entertained.

It was at this time that the condom made its come-back. For most people of my generation, it was an archaic type of contraception and prophylaxis. Our contraceptive had been the pill. As for sexually transmitted diseases, they were common, especially among my male-loving male friends, but for some time now they had not been life-threatening. Even if syphilis is active to this day—and often associated with HIV—we tend to forget the ravages it caused for so long. My father, born in Russia in 1907, would often tell me how lucky we were, because in earlier days syphilitics had to choose between suicide and a ghastly end, whereas for my friends catching it was of little consequence. In the 1970s, other infections such as the clap and various yeast infections had spread quite widely among us, so much so in fact that one day we were obliged to organize a collective medical visit to get treated for some genital condition or other. Imagine the faces of the medical staff of Institut Tarnier when confronted by a gaggle of a dozen or so young men and women with over-lapping and multiform sexual relationships, all of them in consequence having contracted the same venereal disease. By the 1980s, however, we had gained a few years' worth of common sense and lost some of our impulsiveness, which meant that the advent of AIDS and obligatory condoms really stunned us.

All the same, we simply had to comply with the new constraints this foul virus imposed. I was very close to Paul, with whom I worked a good deal, and we also enjoyed many walks, outings and trips together. As a result I was witness not only to the difficulties he faced in dealing with his treatments but also to the advances in the treat-ments themselves. First there was AZT, then combination therapy, and eventually triple therapies. It was hard for him, frustrating and laborious, but Paul always managed to keep it together by dint of courage, persistence, and self-discipline.

Early on, back in Marseille, friends from the old days like Coco began dying. Little by little the extent of the disaster dawned on us. In France the plague spread to people who had hardly even dabbled with heroin; in

Africa, meanwhile, whole populations were being deci-
mated. Many women and men who had enjoyed a rich
and varied sexual life, like me, did not escape. I was lucky.

In tandem with the sinister and indeed deadly hepatitis C, HIV became a familiar specter haunting our daily
lives. So when, at the beginning of 2000, I met Sophie, who
had fallen prey to both of these calamities but dared not
reveal it to anyone but her family, it was easy enough for
me to help her overcome her shame. But I never succeeded,
as close as we became, in getting her to stick to her treatment plan. As a result, like many of my friends who had
"played darts"—as she used to say to avoid the word *needle*—
Sophie died. On a twenty-fourth of December. I have never
really gotten over it.

It would perhaps have made sense for me to join
AIDES—the organization founded in 1984 by Michel
Foucault's partner, Daniel Defert, to combat HIV and viral
hepatitis—or, later on, ACT UP. But AIDES was overshad-
owed for me by its link with Foucault: it represented a
group of left-leaning professors more interested in helping each other than joining the wider struggle, which
was repugnant to me. Paul, who had been close to AIDES
for a while, did nothing to change my mind. As for ACT
UP, its combativeness and its spectacular actions would
have been more my cup of tea, though still far removed
from my conception of revolutionary struggle. But ACT
UP embraced "outing" as part of its strategic arsenal, and
Paul had convinced me that revealing the homosexuality
of well-known figures, whatever one might think of them,
was a despicable act. These days I would say that while the
injunction "Out of the closet!" may be an effective strategy, it is certainly not an admirable one. Except when it is
used against a clear enemy, as when ACT UP threatened

to disclose the homosexuality of a right-wing parliamentarian who dcmonstrated against the PACS law without objecting in the slightest way to the homophobic slogans being chanted.*

I would have preferred to see the fight against AIDS waged under a more global and more radical banner, after the fashion of the early FHAR. Not that I have any complaint about self-defensive struggles, but their methods are simply not mine.

All the same, there were occasions when my anger banished my reservations, as on the night when Paul and I went and daubed vengeful graffiti on the windows of a dozen Benetton stores because the company had used the image of a dying AIDS victim to advertise its sweaters.

Thinking about Sophie's sad death, I am still convinced that, even if the advent of pre-exposure prophylaxis, for example—a preventative strategy based on the continued use of an anti-HIV medicine before or after sexual relations—can stem the worst of the AIDS pandemic's devastation in Western countries, we are far from the end of this catastrophe on the global level. Nor do I doubt that many other such calamities await us in the future, not least the proliferation of powerful drugs with dangerous consequences beyond measure.

Far be it from me to campaign against drugs, which I am certainly ill placed to do, but I cannot talk about AIDS and hepatitis without mentioning heroin. In the late 1960s, the youth of Marseille could get as much as they wanted cheap, thanks to leaks from the local laboratories that processed the substance. The children of

---

* A PACS (Pacte Civil de Solidarité) is a legal union between two people of either sex; it was instituted in France in 1999.

chemists and laboratory technicians, young assistants or others involved in this lucrative export business were able to purloin the substance and push it locally. The cops apparently turned a blind eye as part of their efforts to trace upstream operations in cooperation with their US opposite numbers, whose arrival in Marseille was instantly an open secret. People often say that Marseille is a village. Of course, everyone in France saw Gene Hackman as a freewheeling NYPD cop in *The French Connection*, but natives had spotted his models long before; even I had the American detectives pointed out to me when they were snooping around in our vicinity.

In any case, heroin had flooded the whole region, and the first death by overdose was that of a girl in a bathroom at the Bandol casino. In Aubagne a dealer was said to have obtained his supply from the children of a family who had bought a villa at auction that had previously been used as a laboratory. The father supposedly came across a large bag of white powder and set it aside, meaning to take it to the police, but his children helped themselves to a large quantity without him noticing. All I can say is that I got to know his two sons later on and they were both junkies.

A fair number of comrades got hooked on junk. There were accidents and deaths and then, ten years later, HIV took its toll on the survivors, to be followed in turn by hep C. What happened in Marseille foreshadowed the great wave that swept away a swath of the youth of France and elsewhere. I was very fortunate in that I had little liking for heroin and preferred not a few other drugs that suited me better.

The Coming of Normalization

In 1967, in Aix-en-Provence, we organized a wedding between two young men. Nothing was lacking: the bride's white dress, the groom in tie and tails, a procession of bridesmaids and bridesboys in evening dress, tuxedos, operettish military uniforms and romantic costumes à la Byron. I was compressed into an ancient dress designed by the couturier Paul Poiret, or so said the friend who had taken it for me from the attic of his grandmother— who must have been significantly more lissome than me. I spent the afternoon working on makeup, fixing hairdos, and adjusting falsies. As night fell we processed raucously down Cours Mirabeau to the site of the service, which was presided over by a fake bishop in an amaranth chasuble. The revelry that followed did all the pomp and circumstance justice. In a nutshell, we created a sensation and a scandal. What matter if the groom flew the coop six months later with an antique dealer—and if the bride took this very badly and, according to Jimmy, still had it stuck in his craw long afterwards—what matter, because we achieved our goal, which was to mock the institution of marriage and have fun doing it.

How could we ever have imagined that a time would come when gay men and women would go and get married in a registry office, or that priests, pastors and rabbis might be found more than willing to bless such unions?

Considering everything, we ought to have foreseen it far sooner than we did. The obstacles faced by the partners of those who had died of AIDS had already led, thanks to the aforementioned PACS legislation in France, to the recognition of free unions. By obviating a survivor's eviction from a shared home, their loss of its contents, and their liability to inheritance tax, the PACS law was clearly a boon for hetero couples who shrank from marriage for whatever reason, but for many a gay couple living together and forbidden to marry, its protection was an absolute necessity.

On another front, namely the rights of hospital patients, legal proxies have long been restricted to family members. Since 2002, a "trusted person" may be designated, but that designation must be made either prior to admission, which is to say prearranged, or upon admission, provided that one is in a condition to make it. Otherwise one can easily find oneself in the situation that confronted my friend Angèle when a barrage by hostile relatives opposed her visiting her female partner, temporarily comatose after a road accident. Once Angèle's partner was discharged, needless to say, the two young women lost no time "PACSing."

Marriage is naturally more useful if one has assets: it is, after all, primarily an economic contract. But such is the symbolic freight of the arrangement that practical, material considerations are often little more than a pretext. Never having worshipped at this particular shrine, I tend to take a dim view of those who take pleasure in doing so. But I would very likely have a different attitude had I not enjoyed the freedom to say no to marriage or indeed had marriage been forbidden to me. So even if I can't help chaffing friends of whatever sex who tie the knot, I can still share in their happiness.

As a rule I don't attend weddings or funerals, but I did find myself taking part in the grand nuptials of two guys I knew. I ran into Frédéric and Serge at a birthday party. They had been living together for ten years. Frédéric told me how, the summer before, the two of them had paid a visit to his mother, a neurotic dipsomaniac, and that things had gone badly. An hour later, blushingly and really quite embarrassed, they informed me that they had some news. Straightaway I answered: "You're getting married, right?"

They were gobsmacked: "How did you guess?"

"Well," I replied, "you live in a house that belongs to Frédéric and you've just bought a place together in Burgundy. So when you told me about Frédéric's mother, I just put two and two together."

We were so many at their wedding that there wasn't enough space in the reception room at the town hall of their village in Burgundy, so the ceremony had to be held outside. Luckily it was a glorious day. Being a smart aleck, I asked the mayor if this was his first homosexual wedding. "Why no, Madame," came back his reply, "it's the third. We married two ladies two years ago and two gentlemen last year." So much for smart!

It was a splendid affair, convivial and lots of fun. Naturally Frédéric's mother was not invited, but Serge's parents were there, radiant. I knew that Serge's mother had had some difficulty accepting the idea of the marriage, even though she had always been happy to have the couple over. By now she had clearly overcome her doubts. As for Serge's father, at the first news of the wedding he had only one comment, but it made his approval quite clear: "Oh well, I suppose I'll have to cough up for the wine." And indeed, thanks to him, we drank like gods all night long. But we couldn't get over our surprise at just how ecstatic he seemed. Serge, like Frédéric, was well past forty-five and hardly fit the profile of a young groom. Later, however, the dad confided in me that, fully aware that his only son was a homosexual, he had long ago abandoned all hope of marrying him off, but now that old and seemingly impossible dream of his had come true. As opposed as one might be to marriage, such sheer delight is hard to resist.

Talk of marriage leads inevitably to the subject of procreation, as witness the second of the five articles of the Civil Code that must be read at every ceremony in France: "The spouses shall together ensure the moral and material orientation of the family. They shall provide for *the education of their children and ready them for the future.*" But procreation is not a given in the case of love between spouses of the same sex. To general astonishment, Lucille, who is a lesbian, was the first of my friends to whelp in the immediate wake of May '68. For this purpose she had picked out a handsome and intelligent genitor, the idea being to maximize the child's advantages, but without giving any sign of her intention to the unwitting guy.

Although little Juliette thus had no father, she did have us—which was not nothing. Seen in this tribal light, parenting may well have its appeal.

Not that I never entertained the idea myself. At the age of twenty-eight, I had been living with Donatien for several years. After an acid trip during which we told each other about our childhoods, we decided to make a baby together. Around us several friends had already embarked on parenthood, and we hoped to find a way to avoid the trap of the nuclear family. But it seemed best to wait a while, not least because in those days birth-control pills were said to cause triple or quadruple births, so we planned to pause for at least three months between my stopping the pill and trying to conceive. I'll spare you the details of the acrobatics demanded by diaphragms that would slip through your fingers, bounce up to the ceiling, or lose their shape. Little by little it dawned on me that we were taking on an enormous responsibility. Wasn't there, after all, something deeply reprehensible about bringing a new human being into a world where the prospect of revolution appeared to be evaporating by the day? Especially when, like Donatien, you reproached your own parents for giving birth to you? I concluded that our wish to reproduce was disgracefully egotistical, and Donatien could only agree. So we gave up the idea and I went back on the pill. We separated three years later and neither of us had children subsequently. Nor did I ever have an abortion. When I consider the ghastly state of this world, I have no regrets and I congratulate myself every day for having spared myself the guilt of giving birth.

In the late 1970s, we were a small group of young women loudly rejecting motherhood. We swore not to provide the enemy with either wage slaves or cannon fodder, and if we ever did produce children, we vowed it would only be after the revolution. Of the ten or so we were then, however, only two have remained impenitently childless.

I confess I have never felt an irresistible desire to have a life grow in my belly, to give birth, to suckle, and to experience all the sensations described by some women as gratifying. I have always found it hard to relate to such feelings and tended to ascribe them to social pressures and imperatives. Yet I love children, I am delighted when my girlfriends produce them, and no doubt, had it been easier to do so and had my life been less disorderly, I would readily have adopted some.

Given this attitude of mine, no wonder all the debates over fertility treatments and surrogacy perplex me. I cannot embrace the idea of some right to children that merely echoes a woman's supposed duty to reproduce. As we all know, social pressure in this regard is powerful, and it is not easy to be a refusenik where motherhood is concerned. What is more, I realize that the wish for children is not an exclusively female matter: I have known men to beg a reluctant partner for a child and others who admit forming a couple mainly in order to become parents. But while I can understand a biological desire for parenthood, the application of technology to reproduction makes me uneasy, even though I have not shared my unease with young friends who have resorted to such methods. In today's world getting knocked up is not what it was: the former connotation of pregnancy coming as a surprise—or even as a curse!—is virtually obsolete.

But what is to be done when you are infertile or have no sexual relations with the so-called opposite sex? Things would be so simple if arrangements could be made with friends or family members. This does happen on occasion, and it can work to some degree. Louis and Marthe were an anarchist couple who belonged to my parents' naturist association, and, like quite a few anarchists, Louis had had a vasectomy. But then suddenly Marthe began longing for a baby. So they asked a "comrade" to help out, and the upshot was little Jean-Pierre. At least that was what I was always told. Now, Louis had a brother, Raymond, as much a Stalinist as Louis was an anarchist. Raymond and his wife, Antoinette, were also naturists; they already had two older boys when a little girl arrived, Nathalie, born soon after her cousin Jean-Pierre. Recently, with Raymond and Antoinette long out of the picture, along with Louis, Marthe, and Jean-Pierre, Nathalie asked me whether her father, Raymond, had not perchance also been Jean-Pierre's biological father. Which, after all, was not implausible and would simply mean that the official account had been cleaned up to avoid family complications.

It is easier anyway for a woman with a fully functioning womb to get herself pregnant directly or to procure sperm than it is for a man to find a woman in his circle willing to let herself be inseminated and then hand the result over to him nine months later. In the world of capital, where everything is bought and everything is sold, is it really any worse to rent the uterus of a woman than to exploit her labor power? By the way, isn't it time for the Catholics to come clean and let us know whether their Christ was born by virtue of medical technology, so that Joseph could be the father, or thanks to Mary serving as a surrogate, with Jehovah relying on her belly alone to make himself the dad?

We are a long way from the revolutionary character of homosexuality as conceived by the FHAR and later by the Homosexual Liberation Groups (GLH), whose sister organization the Feminist Lesbian Group (GLF) argued that lesbianism was revolutionary "because it puts the issue of sexuality back on the agenda, and therefore by extension the issue of society's most fundamental aspects, namely the family, the child, reproduction, and the economy."*

If you think about it, the whole set of problems around procreation turns on the question of the nuclear family, whether the parents are a man and a woman, two men, or two women. In a world at long last communized, in which this (so holy!) family was obsolete, I feel sure there would be no need for doctors or lawyers in order to love one another, have children as and when desired, and raise them collectively.

---

* Mathias Quéré, *Qui sème le vent récolte la tapette* (Sow the wind, reap fags) (Lyon: Éditions Tahin Party, 2019).

About Sexual Disorientation

The '68 era scrambled sex roles. Whereas in the early Sixties girls dressed like boys, come the Seventies the boys were dressing like girls. One summer when Donatien and I were in Rome, guys in cars were continually trailing us, because as seen from behind, we presented a dual picture of long hair, pink or white pants, and black or purple Indian cotton tops. Not to mention that we both darkened our eyes with kohl, wore Indian jewelry, and carried shoulder bags. Among hetero couples then, there was a tendency to reverse sex roles: it was common for women to go to work and drive while their men stayed at home, did the cooking and housework and cared for the kids, if any. Such arrangements have survived to some extent for some of our generation. But in the end it would be a mistake to look upon all this as truly liberating. Today young men dye their hair, cover themselves with tattoos, and shave their bodies. This does not stop them behaving like macho creeps, just as being a fan of David Bowie, Freddie Mercury, or Prince in the Eighties or Nineties was no barrier to male chauvinism or heterosexism. As for what sociologists call the "mental load" of housework, despite some progress, it still usually falls on the woman in straight couples and very often on one or the other partner in same-sex ones.

My upbringing probably helped me avoid a good many of the social traps and conditioning that preside over women's station and sexual preferences. I have always failed to understand fixed, exclusive, and permanent orientations as related to love. Even as a child I saw how many things were possible in this sphere. I nevertheless find the notion of "conversion" quite absurd: the idea that one fine day you can decide to change your sexual preferences radically and permanently in one direction or the other makes no sense. The issue is freedom of choice, of course, and this certainly has nothing in the world to do with the "corrective rapes" undergone by lesbians in South Africa or Jamaica, for example. Or with the "therapies" to which individuals who are said to have "made a bad choice" are subjected—not to mention all the torture and other horrors that we hear so much about.

Only too often have I run into girls and women in love with gay men whom they desperately hope to seduce and guys who yearn for the love of lesbians who like them well enough but no more than that. Conversely, there are plenty of gay guys and girls forever in pursuit of heterosexuals hermetically sealed against their charms. What could be more absurd than the familiar refrain "If I ever do convert, it will be with you."

True, everyone is bisexual, some continually, others episodically, and yet others only in their heads. But while this may be theoretically correct, real life occasionally gives the notion a run for its money. Take the case of Magali, my friend as far back as Lycée Marcel-Pagnol, who in those days was given the ugly label of *garçon manqué*. Interestingly, the term *fille manquée* is never used to designate either an effeminate boy or a mannish girl. In any case, the suggestion that one's sexuality might somehow be botched or warped I find utterly repugnant. But as I recall, Magali paid no mind—in fact, she took the label as a joke. So it did not come as a big surprise to me when, after a year at boarding school, she announced that she was a lesbian and had a lover named Marie-Claude.

Magali also had a persistent suitor of whom Marie-Claude was very jealous—as indeed she was of everyone around Magali, male or female, to the point where Jimmy nicknamed her "The Dragon." Magali has nevertheless always proved unmovable, as witness the following anecdote. She was about twenty when she developed a vulvar itch. Marie-Claude sent her promptly to a gynecologist, a kind of specialist hitherto unknown to Magali. The doctor laid her on his examining table, put her feet in stirrups, and inserted a speculum. She cried, "Ouch!" and then noticed that the man was having a meltdown: "Why didn't you tell me you were a virgin? I'm so terribly sorry. But I can mend it—just a little suture." He was falling all over himself with apologies and contrition. Magali did what she could to reassure him: "Doctor, I'm a lesbian, and I don't give a damn for all this stuff about virginity. It's just not important, I swear, and you have nothing at all to fear from me." This earned her a free consultation, and she was still laughing wildly when I joined her a little later.

"Getting myself devirginized with a gynecological gizmo!" she exclaimed. "I can hardly believe it myself."

"The word is *deflowered*, Magali, and the gizmo is a speculum."

"Who cares! I'm the only person this kind of stuff happens to! You should have seen his face. An uptight bourgeois, completely panicked, and me trying to calm him down!"

It was comical, sure enough—and the loss of her hymen was obviously no big deal for Magali, who so far as I know has still never slept with a man.

Love as a passion is truly mysterious and reserves surprises for us that can be truly startling. Take Pascale, for example, a childhood friend of mine who seduced Claudia, a married woman who had never made love to anyone but her husband. Claudia then left the husband, and the two women loved each other and lived together until Pascale died. You could reasonably argue that Pascale *revealed* Claudia to herself. As much could certainly not be said of Daniel, a coworker friend in the late 1970s. Daniel was thirty-five and a confirmed homosexual. You might even have called him *notoriously* homosexual were the phrase not so offensive (because who has ever heard of a *notoriously* heterosexual person?). But one day Daniel informed us that he and Bernadette, who also worked with us, were going to get married and start a family. When I opined that this proposal might not work out well because he would sooner or later meet a man and run off with him, this was his reply: "I love someone and it happens to be a woman. What am I supposed to do?" What more eloquent way to say that "Love is a gypsy child who has never known a law"? And indeed, in fairy-tale fashion, Daniel and Bernadette married and had four beautiful children.

Another surprising instance concerns a thirtysomething straight couple, friends of ours, who hooked up with another couple living with their little boy on the floor above them. The father was attracted to other men, certainly much more than he was to women—except, he claimed, for his wife. The arrangement was fatal for both couples, because the two men fell in love and embarked on a tumultuous affair that lasted so long they both wound up burned out—and single.

More generally, many of us, homo or hetero, have experienced our bisexuality either continually or only at certain moments in our lives. A young man once asked Jimmy an odd question, by text message no less: "Are you bi, gay, or homo?" To which Jimmy replied, more or less: "For a long time I was bi, then I was gay, and now I am mostly affectionate."

Upon learning that Magali's lover, Marie-Claude, had ended up marrying Magali's father and that a member of our tribe had left his wife and children for a young man, my father remarked with flawless logic: "Decidedly, you can't trust anyone"—a characteristically brief summary of the variable geometry of sexual inclination.

Over my lifetime I have made love with hundreds of men but with barely more than ten or so women. While I have known a lot of lesbians and been close to a fair number, I have made few conquests among women who prefer other women as sexual partners. I was once told that I was "too masculine for some and too feminine for others." It is true that my close lesbian consorts—Magali, Lucille, and Pascale—have tended to be butch, and my friendships with them resembled my friendships with men. In general I don't sleep with friends. In love I have always sought the unknown, the uncharted—affairs where you never know if they will last five hours, five days, five weeks, or five years. If I see a man more than three or four times and we develop an affinity, then we become friends. Jokingly, I describe such relationships, depending on the case, as "regimental buddies" or "boarding-school girlfriends." This goes for both males and butch lesbians. As for "feminine" lesbians, I am of no interest to them, even if I telegraph my attraction. No wonder most of my female lovers have been bisexual.

And yet it is with women that I have had my longest love stories—affairs that did not include so-called sexual relations. Ever since childhood I have always had a "best

Traveling with Agathe in Portugal, 1995

girlfriend." For such a soul sister I am ready to do anything, always looking to please her, to protect her, to see her happy, and to forgive her things I would never forgive a man. To the point where one day my bestie Agathe had to rebuke me for being too indulgent and conciliatory towards her and trying to anticipate her slightest whim; she added that "Spats are the spice of friendship" and told me to stop trying to avoid them. This call to order, which I found laughable in the moment, was clearly meant to prevent our relationship from foundering under the weight of routine and the easy compromises that are the death knell of durable love affairs. As Agathe regularly reminds me, "In your life men come and go but I remain"— and it's true enough, because our bond has lasted since 1969, albeit with ups and downs, and we are an old couple even if our relationship is now a long-distance one.

Since my youth plenty of other women have made my heart beat faster, but only with a few did I ever get past the initial enthusiasm of love's earliest moments, when you endow a person you have just met with every conceivable quality and virtue. This reassures Agathe, who unlike me makes no secret of her jealousy, even if in the end she grows to like those I choose, who tend to remain solid friends long after I stop making sheep's eyes at them.

To define myself as bisexual seems reductionist. I prefer to describe myself as polyamorous, with or without sexual relations, meaning that I refuse to distinguish between what is "sexual" and what is not.

My most cherished wish, however, is that any need to claim a particular sexual orientation should disappear. That we should simply love individuals in their difference. But this cannot happen without the abolition of not only the exploitation of labor, not only the institutions of the couple, the family, and normal and normative sexuality, but also of everything else that in a general way steals and poisons our lives.

The Great Degendering

When I was young I met a good many transvestites, but like Lady Jane they cross-dressed by night or onstage only. In the clubs we would occasionally run into the trucker-style male cross-dressers known as *travelos*, forerunners of some of the more flamboyant drag queens of today. I got to know one of them who went by the name of Berthe—as in Bertha Broadfoot—in a club in Saint-Germain-des-Prés. One night when the two of us were fixing our faces in the ladies' room, Berthe began hitting on me, trying to show me how she was also a man and then seriously crossing the line. Getting raped by a *travelo* in the toilets of a gay bar was such an improbable prospect that I was overcome by a fit of the giggles, which prevented me from putting up a serious defense. I was rescued in the nick of time by two lesbian friends who couldn't believe their eyes.

With my deep voice and extravagant getups, I was at times in my youth mistaken for a transvestite; naturally I played along, to everyone's great amusement.

Later on, I was sometimes the only female in political collectives, which is not surprising, because although women are always numerous and active in revolutionary moments, not least in the May 1968 uprising, we have unfortunately been very few until recent times when it comes to developing political theory, to writing and publishing. In one such group I pointed out to a comrade who was lamenting the absence of women that I at least was present, to which he replied, "But you are a man." The thought was reiterated a few years ago when a feminist militant accused me of being "a man in a woman's body."

As ambiguous as I might seem, however, I am definitely female in every way, and not at all unhappy about it. More than happy, indeed, to have achieved control over procreation and to be endowed with one more pleasure-giving organ than a man.

By contrast, I have had female and male friends who cultivated their androgyny: boys who made themselves up and borrowed my dresses and hats, girls who wore shirts and ties, trousers and suits, or bulky jackets over darted pants. Rebecca taped her breasts down to go to the synagogue with the men; Roland became Rolande at the drop of a hat.

Actual transition is another story. There was a young man working at Le Paradou, chic and graceful, a law student at Aix. It seemed to us that he liked to keep a low profile, which was why the ever-inventive Jimmy nicknamed him "Clandestine" and everyone called him Clandès. Five years later, in Paris, I was having dinner in a restaurant with friends when out of nowhere a beautiful, tall, slim mixed-race woman appeared who looked as if she had just escaped from a fashion parade. She hugged me enthusiastically. I was delighted and flattered, but completely foxed. At which the glamorous creature cried, "But honestly, Lola, don't you recognize me? I'm Clandestine, I've left the South and the law behind. I'm called Galia now and I'm a dancer at Le Carrousel!" Not long ago I learnt that Galia went on to preside over Paris-by-night and that in her book, *Quand j'étais petit garçon* (When I was a little boy), she mentioned her sometime nickname of "Clandès" but had apparently forgotten that it was Jimmy who had given it to her.

In the 1980s, Agathe and I used to hang out with a bunch of Brazilians, many of whom were what I call *hommes-fleurs*—always playing games with gender boundaries. After their visit to Paris, the androgynous group Dzi Croquettes left behind a fabulous personage in the shape of Reginaldo. Reginaldo was continually performing, whether onstage or on the town. He was liable to wear a boa over a smoking jacket, an enormous necklace and actor's makeup with a suit, or a Borsalino fedora with a frilly blouse. Lively and cheerful, with a sometimes ferocious sense of humor, for a time he ran a restaurant near the Beaubourg museum with great flair. There we shared *cachaça*, *feijoada*, or *moqueca* with Brazilians, Cape Verdeans, and Angolans, some of them anonymous, others well known, like the singer Bonga, or Luiz Antonio and Rolando, a duo known as Les Étoiles. One morning Reginaldo was found decapitated in his home, his head carefully wrapped in a bath towel. He had most likely been cruising, as he used to do, in the vicinity of Les Tuileries and the Palais-Royal and run into a notorious serial killer of gays who operated according to a set ritual.

In Reginaldo's restaurant and at the dances and parties that he took us to, we saw sumptuous creatures transiting through who made the men fall over themselves; it was hard for them to acknowledge that these splendid women had once been, or so it seemed, little boys. For us they were a delight, and their femininity, far more emphatic than our own, was in our eyes without peer. It is worth recalling that I had a good schooling in such matters from my mother, who one day as she greeted two young women was surprised to hear one of them say to her, "But Génia, don't you recognize me? I am Martine Dubois." Without missing a beat, my mother replied, "Why, of course, you are Geneviève's sister," even though we had known Martine as the young Martin, elder brother of the said Geneviève, a chubby little lad always snuggled between his mother's legs—and I say "legs" because in naturist colonies you don't see a lot of skirts. So Martin had become Martine and was living with a nice young woman. My mother, who had loved Martin very much, grasped the situation instantly, and of course Martine was thrilled.

All the same, a successful legal sex change calls for a fighter, be they male or female. What I know about this I gleaned mainly from Hélène Hazera, the former Gazoline from FHAR days. When Hélène began her transition, she was a candidate in the highly competitive entry exam for the Institute for Advanced Cinematographic Studies (IDHEC). Her candidacy ended as soon it became known that she was transgender. Since she was also obliged to leave the family home, since she had to survive, since hormone treatment was expensive, and doubtless too on account of a strong dose of provocativeness and a salaam to Genet's *Our Lady of the Flowers*, she took a room in Pigalle and started turning tricks. A friend who paid her a visit told me that the silver-jacketed bound edition of the Situationist International's journal and a copy of Vaneigem's *Revolution of Everyday Life* had a place of honor in her room. I cannot say whether her customers appreciated such expressions of theoretical rigor and radicalism, so unlikely, to say the least, to be lying at a prostitute's bedside. Later on, Hélène worked as an irreverent television critic for *Libération* under the bylines HH, Miss HH, and, finally, Miss HH007. Later still, the highbrow radio station France Culture took her on

to host *Chansons dans la Nuit* and then *Chansons Boum*.
She was at times an actress and a producer, and always
a great promoter of books, films and most of all music,
especially Arabo-Andalusian music. Hers has been a life
seemingly easy and comfortable, especially as compared
with that of many other transgender people. The fact is,
however, that without formal changes to one's identification papers, there is a mass of hurdles to confront. How,
for instance, can one claim a piece of mail at the post office
if one's ID does not match one's physical appearance? Not
to mention all the insults, trivial or serious, that this sort
of discrepancy provokes. The last straw came for Hélène
when she applied for her pension and a large portion of it
was withheld on the pretext that she had altered her social
security number illegally by changing the 1 (for male) to
a 2 (for female), even though she had duly informed the
authorities about her transition. Hélène was well known
and had connections, so her problem sparked an uproar
and her rights were restored. One can only hope that cases
like hers help get equal treatment for transgender men or
women without her resources. At any rate, Hélène fights
relentlessly for the most vulnerable among them.

These days gender confusion and transsexuality are
easy pickings for the media—with mixed results, to be
sure. Only too often some idiotic journalist will ask questions such as "What was your first name when you were
a man?" of someone who has never thought of herself as
a man, or show before-and-after photos accompanied by
stupid speculations about a procedure of which they know
strictly nothing. The hard fact remains that trans women
are treated as outcasts and regularly murdered in every
corner of the world. When it comes to getting a job, it is
best to have papers that identify you officially as either a

man or a woman, and obtaining them is of course a nightmare. Before Hélène could get appropriate ID, she had to justify her choice of forename, which struck me as particularly outrageous since her first name is quite ordinary.

Anyway, from where I sit the life of a transgender woman seems grotesquely hard in so many respects. Everyone knows what horrors little girls trapped in a boy's body must endure at school. When you get on in years, when you are no longer the beautiful young woman you once were and your body and face become somewhat more masculine, it seems to me that a trans woman has a much harder time than a postmenopausal "female by birth." And I find it scandalous that there are feminists who refuse to accept trans women as women at all on the spurious grounds that they have not experienced the oppression that they themselves have.

Transition per se seems far from simple. Once I was with Agathe at Carmen's, a late-night bar in Rue Vivienne. We struck up a conversation with a young thing who was clearly not yet a complete woman. Agathe asked for her name, and she was embarrassed: "Do you mean my boy name or my girl name?" Rather schoolmarmishly, Agathe replied, "Tonight you're a girl, aren't you? So what use would a boy's name be to you?" Blushing slightly, she then allowed as how her name was Camille. But when we asked her what she did, she told us she worked as the manager— not the manageress—of the fish counter at a Leclerc supermarket. Not quite ready for prime time, this kid! A few months later I ran into Camille at Carmen's again. She threw her arms around me and had me admire her slit evening gown from Chez Tati, beneath which budding breasts were discernible. The butterfly had emerged from the cocoon. But it had meant losing her job, and she chose to dodge my questions about how she was making ends meet.

One night in the 1980s, in a Marseille bar, I bumped into an old friend whose transition was seriously underway. She led me into the alley behind the place to show me her pretty brand-new tits. Rather stupidly, I asked about the fate of her male genitals, and she responded proudly, "Are you crazy? They work fine, and if they didn't what would happen when I wanted to sleep with a girl?" The sweet thing certainly became a trans woman, but she held firm to her sexual diversity: although she subsequently shared her life with a woman for a very long time, she never gave up cavorting with men.

As for boys born in a girl's body, I don't know much. I have known a good many butch lesbians but none who has undergone hormonal treatment or undertaken breast reduction. It is true that sex-reassignment operations were introduced much later for female-to-male than for male-to-female cases. While Coccinelle was a household name in France as early as the 1950s, no "woman" in those days, so far as I know, ever went further than cross-dressing. But how beautiful and exciting those androgynous women were, whether resolutely lesbian like Claude Cahun or deliciously bisexual like Marlene or Greta!

I am one of those people, women and men, who would like to have no permanent or definite sex, to choose to be whomever they want whenever they want. One of my favorite novels, Ursula K. Le Guin's *The Left Hand of Darkness*, describes a planet where an individual's sex may change arbitrarily. When the book was published in 1969, it caused us to dream, as it seemingly did others too, because it met with great success, garnered prizes, and became a sci-fi classic.

Intersexuality might thus seem very desirable. But I don't believe in reincarnation, so I know I have no chance of being reborn as a snail. And whenever I happen to say that something or someone is breaking my balls, my Agathe is always there to call me to order: "You're dreaming—you don't have any!" To be born a hermaphrodite or intersexual is appealing only in the most abstract way: such a fate usually leads only to persecution and suffering, even if in some cultures being intersex or transgender may confer a particular social role. We must hope, let me say it again, that a day will come when such differences are seen as mere variations in a world that has "changed its foundations," where nobody has to fight for the recognition of a sex any different from any other. To be inter or trans, *hijra* in India, *ladyboy* in Thailand, *rae* in Polynesia, lesbo, queer, bisexual, or a cisgender woman or man will be perfectly insignificant, and there will only be individuals. If this dream ever comes true, I certainly won't be around. Too bad for me, but at least I shall have fought for it.

On Homosexual Communitarianism

The first period of my generation's revolt against sexual repression in France, the time of the 1968 uprising and the FHAR, was part of a global struggle that was collective and in no way compartmentalized. The issue was not the liberation of women and homosexuals alone but a struggle for the emancipation of all. The emergence of the Homosexual Liberation Groups (GLH) and the institutionalization of feminism sounded the death knell of this fine project by ushering in the era of identity politics.

It was in 1981, in San Francisco with Agathe, that I first fully grasped the scope and limitations of gay communitarianism. At that time gays had established their own neighborhood in the Castro District and a horde of young men had poured in from all over the United States and even farther afield to join this joyful homosexual ingathering.

In 1978, Harvey Milk, the first openly gay member of the San Francisco Board of Supervisors, and the city's mayor, George Moscone, had been murdered by Dan White, a disgruntled antigay ex-supervisor. As an activist in the struggle for homosexual rights, Milk knew that his life was at risk. He recorded a kind of audio testament: "If a bullet should enter my brain, let that bullet shatter every closet door." That he had accepted the idea of dying under the banner of coming out helped turn him into a martyr in the gay struggle.

Dan White's trial took place the next year and resulted in a lenient seven-year-and-nine-month prison sentence based on his diminished-responsibility defense that he was suffering from a depression that led him to eat sugary junk food, which in turn affected his behavior. The verdict precipitated a night of violent rioting and violent repression.

Agathe and I were told that after marching to City Hall and trashing the City Center that day, the protestors had withdrawn to the Castro, where some comrades had started to attack a bank branch only to be restrained by others on the grounds that the bank was an integral part of "the community"—that it was "our bank." Which spoke volumes about the said community's ignorance of the power of capital. The fact remains that the United States had now experienced its second serious homosexual uprising, the first being the several days of rioting in Greenwich Village in 1969 that followed the police raid on the Stonewall Inn, a bar "patronized by white, Black, and Hispanic homosexuals too young or too poor to drink elsewhere."*

It was during that same stay of ours in San Francisco that we met with a contretemps slightly reminiscent of my encounter with the Gouines Rouges years before. A young English comrade had invited us to a party at a house where he lived with a "gay anarchist" community. When we arrived we found nothing but men, but since Agathe and I appeared to be a female couple, which we indeed were in large part, we never imagined that we might not be

---

* Cited in Gilles Dauvé, *Homo: Question sociale et question sexuelle de 1864 à nos jours* (Le Mas d'Azil, France: niet!éditions, 2018). English translation and modification: *Your Place or Mine? A 21st Century Essay on (Same) Sex* (Oakland: PM Press, 2022).

welcome. Our host was nevertheless soon obliged to escort us elsewhere, having been rebuked for inviting women to the affair. He was astonished, and so were we.

This might well have remained nothing more than an exotic memory for us were it not for the fact that, once back in Paris, we witnessed the neighborhood of the Marais turn into a "gay community" ghetto where homosexual men far outnumbered lesbians—or, more recently, had not new feminist groups proliferated in France whose exclusionary policies vis-à-vis men put the genteel attitudes of the good old MLF or the Gouines Rouges in the shade.

Today, among "activists," issues surrounding so-called sexual identity have an ever more important place. The acronym LGBT is incessantly being lengthened so that everyone can have their own particular category. First of all, Lesbian/Gay/Bisexual/Trans was supplemented by Q for Queer, then by a plus sign to represent intersex and pansexual individuals, etc., etc. In the United States, the inventory seems endless: the T for Trans subdivides into T for Transgender and Transsexual; the I for Intersex is followed by an A for Asexual, another A for Ally (a hetero supporter of the cause), and finally a P for Pansexual; the Q may stand for either Queer or Questioning; an O for Other seems inevitable.

In "militant" circles, gender identity and orientation identity are paralleled by "race" identity, with all three forms taking priority over class identity. If you are a cisgender male, i.e., a heterosexual whose gender identity corresponds to the sex assigned at birth, you belong on the bottom rung of the identitarian hierarchy, and if you are a bricklayer, say, you will be looked upon as less admirable than any woman, even if she is a Google executive, or any boss of yours who happens to be Black or to have an Arabic-sounding name; if that boss also happens to be gay, you may as well crawl under the table. Let me stop there, because after all the probability of a boss or a boss lady being trans is still infinitesimally low (though I fervently hope not for long).

Fortunately all this goes on in a social microcosm largely under the sway of academia; were it not so, it would be tragic.

As for gay communitarianism, as unrevolutionary as it may seem, we cannot forget that it was forged in response not only to repression but also to the AIDS epidemic. The ubiquity of homophobic violence and the murder of trans-gender people everywhere in the world can hardly be said to challenge the justness of its cause.

The fact is that such defensive struggles are more necessary than ever, but all the same, issue politics should in my opinion never be more than a stage—or rather an aspect—of the struggle against all forms of oppression.

Never Quit!

All in all, the hardest thing has been never giving up. How to achieve this was not so obvious in the 1980s, that damnable decade when every effort was made to rein in all our dreams of the 1970s. True, the prospect of revolution was receding, and I myself had to take a regular job and move into a small rental apartment, but there was never any question of my throwing in the towel, even if I had to be satisfied in the main with collaborating on publications, helping to organize meetings, and seeking out allies. My friends and I were determined not to get rusty. This led, for one thing, when I found a new lover, to our vow to commit some illegal act, together or separately, every day. We honored this pledge for about six months, pilfering, scamming, or dining and dashing, but eventually our energy and imagination began to dwindle. When I was reduced to running red lights, I figured the time had come to slow down. Even if we had begun this purely as a romantic game, it certainly stimulated us and saved us from paralyzing apathy.

These days my friends and I have inevitably grown older, but we can still cook up collective actions, throw big parties, and protest in the streets. We have not given up, and we are not tired. We continue to open our big mouths, we are not about to die on our knees, and we intend to check out at a time of our own choosing.

The proof that we are alive and kicking is that we have lots of young friends. Among them, naturally, all sexual flavors are represented. For my own part, I continue to cultivate precious and tender female friendships and to frequent and attract men who love other men. When I was younger, I was called a fag hag. Could it be that the jocular "hag" part is now literally true? As for the once-neutral "fag," it is now almost taboo.

Is there any good reason for me to tell my life story? It would indeed have remained strictly confidential had not Gilles Dauvé interviewed me and had the interview not been published on the website Douter de Tout 21. Entitled "Let's Abolish Sexual Coding: A FHAR Veteran Speaks," it gave an account of part of my life and especially of my spell in the FHAR.* This sparked a request, mainly but not only from young people, to hear more.

---

* "Explosons les codes sexuels! Une ancienne du FHAR parle," Douter de Tout 21, September 2017, https://ddt21.noblogs.org/?page_id=1769.

Old age is often thought to be sad, but for me it has become a fine time for sharing ideas. After writing a first book for which I had others recount their memories of the 1960s,* I decided, as I embarked on my eighth decade, that telling my own story might be of some use. So I have dredged my memory in the hope that revisiting the past might help illuminate our present; if it doesn't, I shall have failed. I want to contribute in some small measure to the struggles of today by exposing the strengths and weaknesses of the struggles of the past, and to contest fragmented identity politics in favor of "all for one and one for all." Which is my way of continuing to challenge the ruling order.

---

* *Voyage en outre-gauche*; see note on page 61.

My Revolutionary
Fag Hag Friend

I got to know Lola through
the FHAR. A mathemati-
cian lover who was vainly
trying to masculinize me
took me to the apartment on
Rue Charlemagne that Lola
shared with friends. There a
great freedom reigned, and
not just sexual freedom. It
was a place where the last
live coals from the furnace
of May 1968 still glowed.

Hélène Hazera in a not-too-
recent photograph

Distinctions must be
drawn. There was the left
with its totalitarian tendencies—Lenin, Trotsky, Ho Chi
Minh, Mao Zedong—but also its contradictions: the gay
movement originated in the Vive la Révolution (VLR)
tendency and in the paper *Tout!*, both of which were of
the Maoist persuasion. Mainstream anarchists, meanwhile,
managed little more than tolerance for sexual differences.
At Lola's place, by contrast, endless discussion was accompanied by the continual entanglement of bodies.

This was the perfect refuge for me, feeling as I did
more and more uncomfortable in my family. We enjoyed
ourselves immensely and listened to every kind of

music—jazz, pop, or great French songs from the likes of Germaine Montero and Colette Magny. I remember a night when a young guy woke everyone up looking for oil to help him sodomize his partner.

Rue Charlemagne became the HQ of a number of radical queens who had joined together within the FHAR to combat the bureaucratization of that movement. Lola lent us dresses and abetted all our excesses. Her energy was phenomenal. Her chief mode of communication was humor, but when she got angry, you had to watch out.

Foucault used to say that homosexuality did not exist until the late nineteenth century, when the word was coined in Germany. The word *lesbienne*, however, is to be found in Brantôme's *Les Vies des dames galantes*, while Saint-Simon resorts to allusions, as when he writes, "He followed the customs of the Greeks but lacked their intelligence," or, "He hunted fur and feather both." Balzac, for his part, describes a reserved section of a prison as "*le quartier des tantes*" (the fairy area).

In *The Communist Manifesto*, Marx and Engels denounced "bourgeois prejudices," but a few years later, in a letter to Marx, Engels made violently homophobic comments. Not so Fourier, the manuscript of whose *Le Nouveau Monde amoureux* (The new world of love) his followers concealed until its publication in 1967, just in time for the free-loving anarchists of 1968. The work contains a magnificent passage in which Lesbians and Spartans meet in the desert to organize a contest about sublime love. In the FHAR, everyone subscribed to Fourier's distinction between "pivotal" love and "butterfly" love—between solid couples and polyamorousness.

Fourier certainly failed to include "fag hag" in his nomenclature, even if he himself was something of a lesbian-loving man. Some women from all social strata, cocking a snook at gay male chauvinists, share their lives and loves with homosexual men. With the advent of AIDS, they also shared their sorrow. One day when the elevator was out of commission, as I climbed the stairs at the Théâtre de Chaillot with the journalist France Roche, she confided in me that she was now alone, all her friends having died of AIDS. Some, like her, joined the fight against the disease. Another woman, who had married a reactionary gay man, led the charge against homosexual marriage out of fear that her husband might marry a guy. In other words, fag hags come in all shapes and sizes. Among them, Lola is a jewel.

Over the decades Lola and I would lose sight of each other, then hook up again. There were those in the FHAR who disapproved of my transition, but whereas one Françoise d'Eaubonne warned me about hormones that supposedly caused cancer, and queer guys gave me the cold shoulder, Lola always treated my shift to Hélène as perfectly normal. She used to come and visit me in Pigalle, and off we would go to paint the town red.

Today, now that everything is commercialized and our liberated zones have shriveled, this book of Lola's is a precious collection of recipes for freedom, a fine guide to combining political activism with personal liberation.

Hélène Hazera

About the Contributors

Lola Miesseroff was born in 1947 in Marseille. Coming of age during the wildness of May 1968, her life has been a trip through experiments in communal living, free love, radical feminism, and oppositional communism. She is the author of *Voyage en outre-gauche* (Voyage through the outer left), collected memories of veterans of the May '68 movement, and, more recently, of *Davaï!*, a genealogical account of her ever-rebellious antecedents.

Hélène Hazera is a trans woman who was a leading light in the Homosexual Revolutionary Action Front (FHAR), founded in 1971, and in the more radical spinoff group Les Gazolines (1972–74). She has acted in and directed films and worked as a television and later a music critic for the daily *Libération* (1978–99). For many years subsequently, as a passionate lover of Francophone and Arabo-Andalusian music, she deejayed regular shows on France Culture radio.

Donald Nicholson-Smith was born in Manchester, England, and is a New Yorker by adoption. A sometime Situationist (1965–67), he has translated many writings of the Situationist International. PM Press has published his translation of Vaneigem's *Revolution of Everyday Life* as well as that of Anselm Jappe's magisterial intellectual biography of Guy Debord. Otherwise, he has Englished works by Henri Lefebvre, Apollinaire, Artaud, and others, and he is responsible for bringing the noir fiction of Jean-Patrick Manchette into the Anglosphere.

ABOUT PM PRESS

PM Press is an independent, radical publisher of books and media to educate, entertain, and inspire. Founded in 2007 by a small group of people with decades of publishing, media, and organizing experience, PM Press amplifies the voices of radical authors, artists, and activists. Our aim is to deliver bold political ideas and vital stories to people from all walks of life and arm the dreamers to demand the impossible. We have sold millions of copies of our books, most often one at a time, face to face. We're old enough to know what we're doing and young enough to know what's at stake. Join us to create a better world.

PM Press
PO Box 23912
Oakland, CA 94623
www.pmpress.org

PM Press in Europe
europe@pmpress.org
www.pmpress.org.uk

FRIENDS OF PM PRESS

These are indisputably momentous times—the financial system is melting down globally and the Empire is stumbling. Now more than ever there is a vital need for radical ideas.

In the many years since its founding—and on a mere shoestring—PM Press has risen to the formidable challenge of publishing and distributing knowledge and entertainment for the struggles ahead. With hundreds of releases to date, we have published an impressive and stimulating array of literature, art, music, politics, and culture. Using every available medium, we've succeeded in connecting those hungry for ideas and information to those putting them into practice.

Friends of PM allows you to directly help impact, amplify, and revitalize the discourse and actions of radical writers, filmmakers, and artists. It provides us with a stable foundation from which we can build upon our early successes and provides a much-needed subsidy for the materials that can't necessarily pay their own way. You can help make that happen—and receive every new title automatically delivered to your door once a month—by joining as a Friend of PM Press. And, we'll throw in a free T-shirt when you sign up.

Here are your options:

- **$30 a month** Get all books and pamphlets plus a 50% discount on all webstore purchases

- **$40 a month** Get all PM Press releases (including CDs and DVDs) plus a 50% discount on all webstore purchases

- **$100 a month** Superstar—Everything plus PM merchandise, free downloads, and a 50% discount on all webstore purchases

For those who can't afford $30 or more a month, we have **Sustainer Rates** at $15, $10 and $5. Sustainers get a free PM Press T-shirt and a 50% discount on all purchases from our website.

Your Visa or Mastercard will be billed once a month, until you tell us to stop. Or until our efforts succeed in bringing the revolution around. Or the financial meltdown of Capital makes plastic redundant. Whichever comes first.

Your Place or Mine? A 21st Century Essay on (Same) Sex

Gilles Dauvé

ISBN: 978-1-62963-945-1
$17.95   224 pages

In a fascinating and radical critique of identity
and class, *Your Place or Mine?* examines the
modern invention of homosexuality as a social
construct that emerged in the nineteenth
century. Examining "fairies" in Victorian
England, trans men in early twentieth-century Manhattan, sexual politics
in Soviet Russia, and Stonewall's attempt to combine gay self-defense
with revolutionary critique, Dauvé turns his keen eye on contemporary
political correctness in the United States and the rise of reactionary
discourse.

The utopian vision of *Your Place or Mine?* is vital to a just society: the
invention of a world where one can be *human* without having to be
classified by sexual practices or gender expressions. Where one need
not find shelter in definition or assimilation. A refreshing reminder that
we are not all the same, nor do we need to be.

*"Do you ever ask yourself why there is so little class analysis applied to the
assimilation of the 'gay movement,' or even of the previously glamorous
and revolutionary 'subcultures' denoted by the word 'queer,' why today's
'activists' are so keen on reformist political strategies, why the current
LGBTQQIP2SAA configuration used to describe the 'gay' or 'queer'
community indicates a factionalization of sexual identity that has become
so inclusive as to become almost meaningless ? I have, and if you have too,
Gilles Dauvé's* Your Place or Mine? A 21st Century Essay on (Same) Sex
is the right book to be holding in your hands."
—Bruce LaBruce

Archive That, Comrade! Left Legacies and the Counter Culture of Remembrance

Phil Cohen

ISBN: 978-1-62963-506-4
$19.95   160 pages

Archive That, Comrade! explores issues of archival theory and practice that arise for any project aspiring to provide an open-access platform for political dialogue and democratic debate. It is informed by the author's experience of writing a memoir about his involvement in the London underground scene of the 1960s, the London street commune movement, and the occupation of 144 Piccadilly, an event that hit the world's headlines for ten days in July 1969.

After a brief introduction that sets the contemporary scene of "archive fever," the book considers what the political legacy of 1960s counter culture reveals about the process of commemoration. The argument then opens out to discuss the notion of historical legacy and its role in the "dialectic of generations". How far can the archive serve as a platform for dialogue and debate between different generations of activists in a culture that fetishises the evanescent present, practices a profound amnesia about its past, and forecloses the sociological imagination of an alternative future? The following section looks at the emergence of a complex apparatus of public fame and celebrity around the spectacle of dissidence and considers whether the Left has subverted or merely mirrored the dominant forms of reputation-making and public recognition. Can the Left establish its own autonomous model of commemoration?

The final section takes up the challenge of outlining a model for the democratic archive as a revisionary project, creating a resource for building collective capacity to sustain struggles of long duration. A postscript examines how archival strategies of the alt-right have intervened at this juncture to elaborate a politics of false memory.

"Has the Left got a past? And if so, is that past best forgotten? Who was it who said, 'Let the dead bury their dead'? Phil Cohen's book is a searing meditation on the politics of memory, written by someone for whom 'the '60s' are still alive—and therefore horrible, unfinished, unforgivable, tremendous, undead. His book brings back to life the William Faulkner cliché. The past for Cohen is neither dead nor alive. It's not even past, more's the pity."
—T.J. Clark, author of *The Sight of Death*

The Revolution of Everyday Life

Raoul Vaneigem
Translated by Donald Nicholson-Smith

ISBN: 978-1-60486-678-0
$20.00   288 pages

Originally published just months before the May 1968 upheavals in France, Raoul Vaneigem's *The Revolution of Everyday Life* offered a lyrical and aphoristic critique of the "society of the spectacle" from the point of view of individual experience. Whereas Debord's masterful analysis of the new historical conditions that triggered the uprisings of the 1960s armed the revolutionaries of the time with theory, Vaneigem's book described their feelings of desperation directly, and armed them with "formulations capable of firing point-blank on our enemies."

"I realise," writes Vaneigem in his introduction, "that I have given subjective will an easy time in this book, but let no one reproach me for this without first considering the extent to which the objective conditions of the contemporary world advance the cause of subjectivity day after day."

Vaneigem names and defines the alienating features of everyday life in consumer society: survival rather than life, the call to sacrifice, the cultivation of false needs, the dictatorship of the commodity, subjection to social roles, and above all the replacement of God by the Economy. And in the second part of his book, "Reversal of Perspective," he explores the countervailing impulses that, in true dialectical fashion, persist within the deepest alienation: creativity, spontaneity, poetry, and the path from isolation to communication and participation.

For "To desire a different life is already that life in the making." And "fulfillment is expressed in the singular but conjugated in the plural."

The present English translation was first published by Rebel Press of London in 1983. This new edition of *The Revolution of Everyday Life* has been reviewed and corrected by the translator and contains a new preface addressed to English-language readers by Raoul Vaneigem. The book is the first of several translations of works by Vaneigem that PM Press plans to publish in uniform volumes. Vaneigem's classic work is to be followed by *The Knight, the Lady, the Devil, and Death* (2003) and *The Inhumanity of Religion* (2000).